AMERICAN SLAVERY

DISTINGUISHED FROM

THE SLAVERY OF ENGLISH THEORISTS,

AND

JUSTIFIED BY THE LAW OF NATURE.

BY

REV. SAMUEL SEABURY, D.D.,

AUTHOR OF "DISCOURSES ON THE SUPREMACY AND OBLIGATION OF CONSCIENCE."

"Atqui nos legem bonam a malâ nullâ aliâ nisi NATURÆ NORMÂ dividere possumus."—*Cicero* De Leg., lib. i., sect. 16.

"CIVIL GOVERNMENT has been, in all ages, a standing publication of the LAW OF NATURE."—*Bishop Butler*, Ser., 1 Tim. ii. 1-2.

NEW YORK:

MASON BROTHERS,

5 & 7 MERCER STREET.

1861.

STEREOTYPED BY
SMITH & McDOUGAL,
82 & 84 Beekman-st.

PRINTED BY
C. A. ALVORD,
15 Vandewater-st.

PREFACE.

The evil of sectional agitation, foreshadowed by the Father of his country, is upon us; and the North and the South are arrayed the one against the other.

One of the sources of our dissensions (in my judgment the original and chief source) is the opinion that has been extensively propagated, that slavery is a *moral* and *social* evil; that is (though the words are not generally used in their full significance), that it is wrong in morals and disgraceful in Christian and civilized society.

The fact that the Constitution of the United States covers Slave States as well as Free, is reason enough, in my opinion, why every man that lives under it should assume slavery to be neither morally wrong nor socially disreputable. Slavery is no more forbidden by Scripture than by the Constitution, but is permitted by both; and I can not but think that modesty and good sense should have taught all citizens and all Christians who could not see the *reason* of the permission, to take it on the *authority* of the Constitution of their country and the Rule of their Faith, without an appeal to a higher law.

It is clearly repugnant to the genius of our government to mix up questions of morality, religion, and social life, with our national politics; and, as slavery, in some of its bearings, is a legitimate and often necessary object of municipal legislation, it is the more to be regretted that it should be complicated with questions of morality, religion, and social reputation. Nevertheless, this has been done; and the natural consequences have followed;—rancor, and hatred, and deeply rooted alienations, such as no merely political discussions could engender.

My aim is to help to withdraw from this vexed controversy, if it be possible, its moral, religious, and social element; that thus slavery, when it is made an object of national legislation, may be discussed and disposed of on merely economical and political grounds.

But to do any thing effectively in this way, it is necessary to take decided ground. The political differences on this subject may be accommodated by mutual concession and compromise, consistently with self-respect. But it is not so with the moral and social question. No bridge of compromise can be thrown over the chasm that separates truth, justice, and honor, from falsehood, injustice, and shame. The relation of master and slave, and the claim of property involved in it, are either just and honorable, or unjust and base; and hence I see no other way to adjust the differences that exist in reference to this phase of the subject than to induce men to examine and decide, on rational grounds, the right or wrong of the question, before they attempt to heal the exacerbations that grow out of it.

The decision to which I am brought on this point, by an investigation as careful as I am capable of making, is adverse to the general sentiment in the Northern States. I hope, however, this will be no bar to an impartial consideration of the reasons on which I shall endeavor to sustain it. With candid and ingenuous minds I am sure it will not be.

And if ever candor and ingenuousness were needful for any persons on any subject, they are needful for us at the North on this subject at the present time. Slavery at the South is an immovable fact, accepted at first from necessity, and cherished now (as its patrons tell us, and I readily believe them), from conviction. With the views which at present prevail on this subject at the North, it is neither desirable nor possible that our Union should much longer continue; not desirable, for antagonistic opinions on a subject of morality, religion, and daily life, must breed constant and rancorous irritation; not possible, for no government, however well-intentioned or however strong, can give permanent effect to laws designed for the protection of slavery, among a free and intelligent people who believe slavery to be morally unjust and socially degrading. The love of country, therefore, the love of peace, the love of liberty for ourselves, our posterity, and for all nations, no less than the love of truth, should persuade us to lay aside the bias of party, our prepossessions in favor of great names, and all our prejudices, that we may calmly and candidly review a subject, which, in the present crisis of affairs, involves more momentous interests than any other of a worldly nature which can occupy our attention.

It has been the singular happiness of the American people to have the greatest facilities and the best opportunities for acquainting themselves with the grounds and real merits of every great national question which has heretofore been submitted to their judgment. Men of unrivaled eloquence and of consummate ability and learning in their respective departments, have thoroughly ventilated each subject of national concern, before the people have been called upon for their ultimate decision. This has been our great security for the principle of self-government, and the chief cause of its success among us. But in the opinions which they have formed, or may form, on the point now presented to them, they have not and can not have advantages of the same kind. Congress may discuss slavery in its economical and political bearings, and the Supreme Court may determine the rights of property involved in it, on grounds of *legal* justice; but they can go no further without transcending their proper functions; and hence the *moral* and *religious* question, which is really in issue before the people, is one which the people are obliged to determine without the facilities which they have had for coming to a right judgment on other subjects of national interest. I mention this as a reason why we at the North should be more ready to suspect the soundness of our past opinions, and why our brethren at the South should have patience, and not mistake the somewhat demonstrative opinions at the North for our deliberate and immutable judgment. True, the anti-slavery storm has raged for thirty years; but what is thirty years in the life of a nation?

With this brief premonition I commend the following work to the public, for whose sake, and not for any private ends, it has been written. By their judgment I shall cheerfully abide. If I am so happy as to carry conviction to my reader's mind, I shall be thankful. If I fail in this end, I shall still have the satisfaction to reflect, not only that I have been actuated by a good intention, but that I have promulgated no sentiments which can array brother against brother, and *make a man's foes those of his own household;* nor indeed uttered a word which can give just occasion of offense either to piety or to charity.

S. S.

NEW YORK, Jan., 1861.

CONTENTS.

CHAPTER I.

CHAPTER II.

CHAPTER III.

CHAPTER IV.

CHAPTER V.

CHAPTER VI.

CHAPTER VII.

CHAPTER VIII.

CHAPTER IX

CHAPTER X.

CHAPTER XI.

CHAPTER XII.

CHAPTER XIII.

CHAPTER XIV.

CHAPTER XV.

CHAPTER XVI.

CHAPTER XVII.

CHAPTER XVIII.

CHAPTER I.

INTRODUCTION.

THE first article of the amended Constitution of the United States declares that "Congress shall make no law respecting the establishment of religion or prohibiting the exercise thereof." This declaration is justly dear to the hearts of the American people. It secures to every citizen the enjoyment of liberty of conscience, or the sacred right to worship God according to the dictates of his own judgment, "with none" on earth "to make him afraid." It puts the various denominations of religion on an equal footing, protecting all but showing preference to none; and thus saves the people from a prolific source of jealousy and discord. The dictate of practical wisdom, it is at once the charter of religious liberty and a preventive of religious dissension.

It would be a great mistake, however, to imagine that this wise provision of the Constitution was intended to effect an absolute severance between government and religion. The law of Nature, or the law founded in the relation of creatures to one another and to their Maker, is the foundation of all just human laws; and the belief of its divine authority and sanction is the most efficacious motive to the observance of these laws, and the most enduring bond of human society. This divine law, the obligation of which has been confessed in all ages and all countries, in opposition to which all human laws are nugatory, and the belief of which underlies every variety of religion, is undoubtedly assumed by the Constitution as the basis of the government which it creates, and the limit of its powers. To this extent the Constitution itself is in alliance with religion, establishing its most fundamental principles, and depending on its power over the minds of the people for support. Hence, the very clause which forbids Congress to establish religion, restrains it also from prohibiting such establishment. "Congress shall make no law *respecting* the establishment of religion," either for or against it. It shall not decree its establishment; for a law of Congress to this effect, would, of necessity, involve the adoption of some religious tenets in preference to others, or an alliance with some denomination to the exclusion of others. Neither shall it forbid its establishment; for this would be to abjure the fundamental principles of all religion and of all just government, and consequently to destroy its own function and to die by its own hand. Congress shall make no law on the subject one way or the other, but shall leave the government to that natural alliance with religion which God himself has made necessary to its health and perpetuity.

If further proof be needed to show that this was the design of the framers of the Federal Constitution, we may appeal, among other evidences to the same effect, to the Farewell Address of Washington, which, from the unanimous approval it has received, is entitled to be regarded as an authorized exposition of their sentiments. For having distinguished a unity of government from a mere league or confederation which would be liable at any moment to be dissolved by accident or passion or other inconsiderable cause; and having insisted on a unity of government as necessary to the welfare and prosperity of the States, the address proceeds to impress on the people the belief that religion and morality are the main pillars of government, and to incite them to the maintenance of a common government from the fact of their agreement in a common religion. "It is of infinite moment," are the words of the Address, "that you should properly estimate the immense value of your NATIONAL UNION to your collective and individual happiness;" and it then adds, as an inducement to the preservation of the Union, "With slight shades of difference you have the SAME RELIGION, manners, habits, and political principles." "Religion and morality," it further declares, "are indispensable supports of all the dispositions and habits which lead to political prosperity." It denies the tribute of patriotism to the man who labors to subvert "these great pillars of human happiness, these firmest props of the duties of men and citizens." It warns the people against the popular fallacy "that morality can be maintained without religion;" and declares "that reason and experience both forbid us to expect that national morality can prevail, to the exclusion of religious principle."

Religion and morality both teach us to abstain from injury, to keep our engagements, and to fulfill the relative duties of life. So far they are agreed and work together in harmony. Considered separately and apart, however, they are essentially different. Mere morality, or morality not founded on religion, permits us to regard the distinction between right and wrong, virtue and vice, as arbitrary and conventional; as having no higher standard than human prescription, no higher aim than the temporal welfare and convenience of society. Religion, on the other hand, teaches that the distinction between right and wrong, virtue and vice is founded in the will of God; that the obligation of men to do what is right and virtuous, and to shun what is wrong and vicious, exists antecedently to, and independently of, all human pacts and covenants, and is in fact necessary and eternal. Thus, what morality recognizes as rules of convenience, religion* enjoins as the laws of God,

* "Religion and morality differ not only in the extent of the duty they prescribe, but in the part in which they are the same in the external work. They differ in the motive; they are just as far asunder as heaven is from the earth. Morality finds all her motives here below; religion fetches all her motives from above. The highest principle in morals is a just regard to the rights of each other in civil

fixed and immutable, and binds on the consciences of men by the fear of God and of judgment to come. Very justly, therefore, are we cautioned (in the Farewell Address) against the delusive fancy that morality can be maintained without religion.

I make no doubt that God has bestowed on every creature its proper nature, and placed it in certain relations from which a rule of action flows, and that this rule is the will and law of the Creator. But the facts of history do not suffer me to believe that human reason is competent to declare this rule with that clearness and authority which are necessary to command the assent and to bind the consciences of the generality of men. This blessing we owe to Divine Revelation, which has not left us to discover our Maker's will either by intuition (which is the proper guide of angels and not of men), nor by the slow and uncertain deductions of reason, but has delivered it to us in plain and authoritative precepts. Hence when I speak of religion, I must be understood to mean revealed religion; and I suppose that the word *religion* is used in the same sense in the Farewell Address.

In this sense it will hardly be denied that religion

society; the first principle in religion is the love of God—or, in other words, a regard to the relation which we bear to Him, as it is made known to us by revelation; and no action is religious, otherwise than as it respects God, and proceeds from a sense of our duty to Him, or at least is regulated by a sense of that duty."—*Bishop Horsley's Charge to his Clergy*, 1790.

is the foundation of human society; the ground on which morality rests for its support and permanence, the source from which it derives its purity and efficiency. As readily will it be allowed that the American people, at the time of the adoption of the Federal Constitution, had one and the same religion. The theory which resolves virtue and vice into social conventionalities, a theory essentially atheistic and subversive of human integrity, was abhorrent to the minds of the people, and has left no trace of its existence in the Constitution and fundamental laws of the Union. The law of Nature, which is only another name for the religion of Nature, has been assumed as the rule of conscience and the basis of legislation; not the law of Nature as dimly apprehended by Pagans and Mohammedans,* or as perverted by wild and infidel theorists, but the law of Nature as declared by Divine Revelation and embodied in the institutions of the Christian religion. Hence the sanction of an oath in order to the discharge of all the functions of government, executive, legislative, and judicial; and that oath administered in the Name of the One God and on the Holy Evangelists. Hence the recognition of Christian marriage as the foundation of the family relation, and consequently of the Christian

* I make no allusion to the Jewish religion, because I regard it as *essentially* the same as the Christian; Judaism being Christianity in the letter, and Christianity being mystical Judaism; that is to say, the Jewish religion in spirit and in truth.

family as an integral element of society. Hence also the absence of all constitutional provisions and fundamental laws which, in the remotest degree, contravene the Christian religion or any of its undoubted requirements.*

Few things, indeed, are more remarkable than the unanimity which Christianity has produced, wherever it has prevailed, in regard to the fundamentals of religion. Differences of opinion, it is true, have always subsisted among men, and probably always will subsist. They arise in part from the constitution of the human mind, which is such that every truth that is lodged in it generates new inquiries, and leads to speculation and conjecture in regard to regions of knowledge yet unexplored and undiscovered. Christians differ among themselves, no less than the ancient Heathen differed. But how unlike, the subject-matter of their differences! The Pagan philosophers differed from one another as to the foundations of all religion, the Being of God, the

* The State of Delaware has expressly acknowledged the Holy Trinity and the Divine inspiration of the Scriptures. The 22d Art. of its Constitution required every person who shall be chosen a member of either house, or appointed to any office or place of trust, before taking his seat, or entering on the execution of his office, in addition to the usual oath of office, to make and subscribe the following declaration, *to wit:*

"I, A. B., do profess faith in God the Father, and in Jesus Christ, his only Son, and the Holy Ghost, one God blessed for evermore; and I do acknowledge the Holy Scriptures of the Old and New Testaments to be given by Divine inspiration."

origin of the Universe, the government of the world by Divine Providence, and the reality of the distinction between good and evil, virtue and vice. Opinions which were then the badges of conflicting sects, and divided the minds of the people, are now for the most part broached only by the few who delight in paradoxes, or who, having dug up some old error, hope to gain a name by proclaiming it to the world as a new truth. In effect Christianity has shifted our differences from the foundation to the superstructure; or to speak more accurately it has brought us to an agreement respecting the system of Nature, and left us to make for ourselves new differences in regard to that system of Redemption which it has pleased God to superinduce upon Nature. In respect to this latter system which revealed religion represents as moving forward to its consummation concurrently with the system of Nature, the differences of Christians are unhappily great and irreconcilable; but in regard to natural religion, *i. e.*, in regard to religion considered as abstracted from the scheme of Redemption, and as limited to the acts and agents of this world, there can be no doubt, I suppose, that the various denominations of Christians, comprising at the time of the adoption of our Federal Constitution the great body of the American people, were substantially agreed.*

* Bishop Gibson, in his second Pastoral Letter to the Diocese of London, A. D. 1760, satisfactorily shows that the people of Great Britain at that time, notwithstanding their multiplicity of sects, were

The time that has elapsed since the adoption of the Federal Constitution, has witnessed some extraordinary and conflicting developments of opinion. The mind of the Northern and Eastern States—surpassed by that of no other age or country in acuteness, activity, and depth, excited by keener stimulants and vaster prospects, and yet thrown upon its own energies with no hereditary institutions to steady it, with no learned order to guide it, except in dependence on popular support (which means subserviency in the end to the popular will), has germinated, as it were, with wild luxuriance, and put forth, among many good fruits, not

united in a rule of faith and practice, embracing the most necessary points of religion. The same statement was probably applicable to their American descendants at the time of their separation from the mother country. The summary is: "That the world and all things in it were created by God, and are under the direction and government of His all-powerful hand and all-seeing eye; that there is an essential difference between good and evil, virtue and vice; that there will be a state of future rewards and punishments, according to our behavior in this life; that Christ was a teacher sent from God, and that His apostles were divinely inspired; that all Christians are bound to declare and profess themselves to be His disciples; that not only the exercise of the several virtues, but also a belief in Christ is necessary in order to their obtaining the pardon of sin, the favor of God, and eternal life; that the worship of God is to be performed chiefly by the heart in prayers, praises, and thanksgivings; and as to all other points, that they are bound to live by the rules which Christ and His apostles have left them in the Holy Scriptures. Here then," he adds, "is a fixed and certain rule of faith and practice, concerning all the most necessary points of religion, established by a divine sanction, embraced as such by all denominations of Christians, and in itself abundantly sufficient to preserve the knowledge and practice of religion in the world."

a few crude theories of morals and religion. In tho prosecution of Moral Reform, Temperance, Anti-Slavery, Woman's Rights, and other fancied schemes of philanthropy, it has contrived to divest some gross sins of their deformity, and to convert, by means of penal enactments, some innocent actions into crimes. In a word, it has proposed for our consideration, and made some progress in forcing on our acceptance, a new church, a new creed, and a new decalogue. In the Southern States, where the distinctions of society are permanent and sharply defined, where the fountains of learning and science are open to the few, and the many are confined to bodily toil and labor, the tone of thought has been naturally more conservative. Slavery, whatever be its real or imaginary evils, like all fixed institutions, unchanged in the midst of changes, has given stability to socicty; it has been, and still is a standing protest against the mental extravagancies of the New England States; and it will probably continue to beat back the waves of Northern fanaticism, unless the deeper and hoarser torrent of Northern cupidity, following the precedents of history, roll down on the South to complete the devastation which Northern fanaticism has begun.

Slavery is at present the great point of antagonism, not so much, I think, between the North and the South, as between order, conservatism, and Christianity on the one hand, and misrule, anarchy, and infidelity on the other. Had the institution been assailed merely on economical and political grounds, there would be nothing to justify this remark. Men may discuss the comparative advantages of free and servile labor, and their respective influences on morals and public virtue, just as they discuss questions of tariff and revenue, and push their discussions, as men are wont, with heat and passion, without endangering the structure of society, or the stability of government. If the opposition to slavery had been rested on these grounds only, it could have done no harm, and might have been productive of good. Had nothing more been done than to stigmatize slavery as "a relic of barbarism," there had been no cause of alarm; for as nations, like men, sometimes die of repletion, and an excess of liberty betokens decay, so time alone can determine whether the South be really retrograding in civilization, or whether its Northern opponents, in vaunting their superiority, be not rather enacting the vanity of the ancient Greeks, or the impudence of the modern celestials. But slavery is not assailed merely on these grounds. It is assailed also on grounds of morality and religion. It is held up, for the first time in the world's history, to the scorn and execration of mankind; not merely for its abuses, but as being in itself a violation of the law of Nature; the law which is the fountain of justice, and in opposition to which no government ought to subsist. It is true, that this opinion is held with various degrees of consistency, and with cunning adaptations to the demands of public expediency, and the whispers of private interest. Some would have the "higher law" (as it is called), or what they fancy to be its dictates, carried out at all hazards, to the extent even of insurrection and treason. Others aim to conform to it by some scheme of gradual emancipation, and by certain yet undefined changes of government. Others, again, distinguish between slaveholding simply considered, and holding slaves with the purpose of emancipating them when Providence shall have opened the way; denouncing the former practice as a sin, and regarding the latter, if I understand them right, as a sin divested of its guilt by the good intention of the sinner. Some are violent, others crafty, and others both violent and crafty; but they are all united in a detestation of slavery as oppressive, unjust, and altogether repugnant to the law of Nature; and, consequently, in either condemning, or justifying only on the ground of a stringent necessity or temporary expediency, all human compacts and enactments which are designed to uphold it.

And it is very observable that while the opponents of slavery assail it as a violation of natural right, they are not met by their antagonists on their own ground. The defenders of slavery entrench themselves behind the law of the land and the Scriptures; but they do not, so far as their arguments have fallen under my notice, defend slavery on the ground of natural right. For the argument founded on the inferiority of the African race does not come up to the point. It rests the relation now subsisting between the races at the South on the ground of an assumed expediency, without affirming its immutable justice; and dominion founded on expediency without, or against justice, is no better than oppression and tyranny. If the existing relation is first proved and confessed to be just and right, then indeed the fitness of the white race for dominion, and of the black for servitude, is a sound argument for continuing the relation, or for not interfering with it where it exists. But the *mere* fitness can not create the relation; can not give the white a just title to dominion, nor make servitude the duty of the black. For the doctrine attributed to the Stagyrite that the Athenians might lawfully invade and enslave any people who, in their opinion, were fit to be made slaves, is, and I hope always will be, abhorrent to the religion of the American people; and if slavery has no better foundation than this to rest on, it deserves to fall; and it is but natural that the energies of a Christian people should be directed, if the way is open, to effect its extirpation.

Moreover, to rest the defense of slavery exclusively on the law of the land and on Scripture, begets the impression that they are not on this subject in harmony with the law of Nature; and the consequence is that the people are led, not only to speak contemptuously of the Constitution for the protection which it extends to slavery, but to disparage the Holy Scriptures also, and to resort to forced interpretations to get rid of their testimony in its favor. The people, indeed, on the whole, are as yet loyal to the Union, and attached to the Christian religion; but they believe, for the most part, that slavery is contrary to natural right (that is, that it is a moral wrong or sin, though they may disclaim the word); and starting with this premise, one of two things will probably follow; either they will pursue successfully one scheme after another, looking to ultimate abolition; or, failing of success, they will become more and more disaffected and averse to all union, political and religious, of which slavery is an element. For the public, in the long run, is a severe logician; and will either abandon its premises, or carry them out to a rigid conclusion.

It seems, therefore, in a manner necessary to bring the question of slavery to the test of the law of Nature; if for no other purpose, at least to remove, if possible, even the semblance of disagreement or collision among laws that are meant to conspire, with a divine harmony, for the good of human society. For no greater calamity can befall a patriotic and Christian people, than a persuasion, even though it be a mistaken persuasion, that either the law of their country or the revealed law contradicts, in any point, the law of Nature, the eternal and immutable rule of the human conscience, which no man can be expected to relinquish, and which the ministries of God in church and state are really designed to develop and confirm. For the law of the land in its legitimate design, and the law of Christianity from an intrinsic necessity, pre-suppose the law of Nature, are declarative of it, and reënforce it with new motives to obedience. They form together, in a normal state of Christian society, a triple cord, binding us together as men, as citizens, and as Christians in the united discharge of all relative duties. To untwist this cord, and to remove one of its strands, is to lay a tension on the others which they were not intended to bear. Is it necessary to do this in reference to slavery? Is not the institution agreeable to the law of Nature, as well as to the law of the land and to the Scriptures? This is the question which I propose to examine.

CHAPTER II.

LAW, JUSTICE, RIGHTS, LIBERTY, SLAVERY: MEANING OF THE WORDS.

As words are the medium of human thought, so it is impossible for men to think clearly on any subject without first distinguishing their meaning, and using them as far as possible in a uniform sense. Great confusion has been caused in the minds of many, on the subject we are about to consider, by a neglect of this precaution; and I shall, therefore, hope for the reader's attention while I endeavor to remove this obstacle by a definition of some of the chief words involved in the discussion. And first for the word *law*.

By *law* (from the Saxon *licgan*, *to lie down*, or more directly from its passive participle *lagu*,* *what is laid*

* Pronounced *lauyu.* Not only in the Saxon, but in the old English, the *g* had a liquid sound like our *y* or *w*. In an old copy which I have of Erasmus on the Creed, A. D. 1533, *given* is spelled *yeven*, and *equal*, *egal;* and the same power of the letter is still seen in the words, *anywise*, *otherwise*, etc., which were written even so lately as the last century, *any guise*, *other guise:* the *wise* in these compounds, not being, as is commonly supposed, a corrupt form of *ways*, but the same as *guise* (which means *mode* or *method*), and preservative of the original pronunciation.

or fixed) we understand a fixed rule directive and operative of good. In its highest form it is a rule which the Divine wisdom lays on itself for its outward manifestation; and in this sense the laws of God are those rules which God has fixed in His own mind for the government of His creatures. In a somewhat lower sense, it is a rule which God has laid on His creatures, directive and operative of the end for which they were created. The end for which all things are created is good; He who created all things infallibly knows the end and the best means of obtaining it; and therefore His laws are necessarily directive and operative of good. Human laws, indeed, so far as they are merely human, and not a transcript of the divine, have necessarily the alloy of human imperfection; yet still they aim at a good end, and what we mean by a bad law is one that fails to accomplish the good for which it was intended. So that divine laws absolutely and in fact, and human laws, in their design and in a certain approximate sense, are not merely rules of action, but rules of action directive and operative of good.

It is well, however, to observe that the laws of God operate in different ways according to the different natures of those creatures on which they are laid. The laws of matter operate on matter according to the nature of matter which has neither sense nor power of self-motion. The laws of the brute creation operate on brutes according to the nature of brutes, which have sense and the power of self-motion, but have neither will nor reason. The laws of human nature operate on man according to his reasonable nature, and in a manner suited to that will which is a part of his reasonable nature: they *oblige*, but they do not *compel*; and hence it happens that, while the laws of God effect necessarily the ends for which they are intended on other creatures, and on man also, as respects his bodily and sensitive nature, they do not work these ends on our reasonable nature without our own concurrence. God himself can not compel an unwilling mind to goodness.

To avoid confusion, it is necessary also to distinguish between *Law* and *Justice*, and to define their relations. The word *justice* is sometimes used to denote an attribute of the Deity; or, to speak more correctly, it is used to denote that absolute and inconceivable perfection in the Divine mind to which the virtue of human justice bears a certain analogy or proportion. In this sense of the word *justice*, the law of Nature is an effect of justice, and is established by justice; because it is an effect of God, and is established by God, whose justice is infinite. In no other way, then, can we determine whether a thing is agreeable or repugnant to the justice of God, than by comparing it with the law of God. This consideration, if attended to, would cut off much idle declamation; for men are apt to conceive of the justice and holiness of GOD after a picture of their own imagining, and then to denounce things as contrary to those Divine attributes, when in truth they are only contrary to the standard which they have set up in their own minds.

But this Divine law which is the effect of Divine justice is itself directive and operative of justice in the minds of men. For justice considered as a human virtue is the constant and perpetual desire of giving to every man his due; a certain habitual rectitude of will, which disposes us to render to others whatsoever we owe them. Sometimes, indeed, the word is used by a metonymy of the effect for the cause, to denote the duty done, as well as the temper which moves us to do it. Thus we say that the justice of the magistrate leads him to hear both sides, and that the justice of men leads them to pay their debts; and we say also that the magistrates dispense justice, and that men in their dealings render justice to one another. In both senses, however, justice is primarily the effect of law; for in the former senses it presupposes law as its rule and guide, and in the latter sense it is that which the law enjoins: *Jus est quod lex præcipit.* For although we may conceive of human justice as existing independently of, and anterior to, human prescriptions and enactments, and as even imitating the Divine justice by framing subordinate rules for its manifestation, yet we can not conceive of it otherwise than as dependent on some law superior to itself: for if we consider it as a temper or habit of mind, we find that it presupposes law, and is guided by it to be what it is; or if we consider it as an act we see that it is that which some law, previously existing, directs to be done. And therefore we say that justice, considered as a human virtue, is primarily and essentially the product of a law superior to itself; of that law which God has laid on all mankind; and which, because it is laid on the human nature, is called the law of Nature. If we speak, then, with reference to the first principles of human action, we are bound to acknowledge that law takes the precedence of justice, and to test our notions of justice by comparing them with that which is the standard of justice, law.

We may consider further that justice is a relative virtue: it has respect not to one's own self and possessions, but to the persons and goods of others. Who, then, can conceive of justice, either as a habit or an act, without previous definition of law?. As long as men are fallible and liable to have their judgment warped by interest, prejudice, or passion, so long will they have differences and disputes. And when arguments have failed, and friendly arbitrations can not be had, how are their differences to be adjusted and their disputes terminated? In no other way, peaceably, than by an appeal to law; to the law of the State on questions of municipal justice: to the law of Nature on questions of universal justice. If they refuse to abide by the law, or can not obtain its decisions, they commonly either accommodate their differences by mutual concession, or appeal to the sword as their final arbiter. *Inter arma silent leges;* in war it is not always justice, but often fortune, or rather Providence, which has further and greater ends to answer than those that respect the merits of the contest, that determines the issue: but while the laws are operative, they are the wells and fountains to which men resort for the distribution of justice.

I do not mean to affirm that this relation is never reversed. Human justice, as already intimated, after the example of its divine prototype, may enact laws; and these laws are of course the effect of justice, and not its cause. In fact most of the laws under which we live are of this nature: hence many persons, drawing, as men are wont, a universal conclusion from a partial truth, are led to suppose that law, simply considered, is subordinate to justice, and has no force against justice; and then having raised justice above law they are naturally and necessarily led to resolve justice into an instinct or feeling, or to make it the product of their own crude notions and fancies; tempted thereto, perhaps, by the old and secret prompting, "Ye shall be as gods!" Whereas, in truth, and this is what I affirm, human justice could not originate laws, could not have an actual or even a conceptional existence, unless it were itself at first originated and guided by laws superior to any and every manifestation of its own. So that, if we trace matters to their source, we find that justice is the offspring of law, as is law the offspring of God.

Hence the founders of States have sought to fortify their constitutions by the sanction of divinity; and indeed (θεοῦ νόμοι) that fundamental laws are of God has been the common sentiment of mankind.

Another notion which it may be well to consider is that of *Rights*—their origin and nature.

The functions of law are to command and to forbid, to permit and to punish. These are the functions of the law of Nature as well as of other laws. Some things it commands; as, to live honestly, and to give to every one his due. Other things it forbids; as, to do injury to any creature. Now, when the law commands one person to render a duty to another, it entitles the latter to demand that duty of the former; that is, it gives him a *right* to exact its performance: for example, the law that commands children to honor their parents, gives parents the *right* to exact honor from their children. Again, when the law forbids us to do some things, it permits us to do other things which are not forbidden; that is, it gives us the *right* to do them. For example, the law which forbids me to walk beyond certain limits, permits me to walk within those limits; in other words, it gives me the *right* to do so. Hence we see the origin and nature of *rights;* which are no more than a power, faculty, or liberty to have or to do. A natural right is simply a liberty that a man has to exact something of another which the law of Nature enjoins that other to render to him; or it is a liberty which a man has to do something which the law of Nature does not forbid him to do. In like manner a civil right is a liberty to exact of others what the civil law requires them to render to us; or it is a liberty to do that which the civil law does not forbid us to do. Rights, therefore, do not oblige. The law may forbid or not permit me in certain cases to waive my rights, and it may oblige and compel me in other cases to assert them. But rights themselves are not laws and have not the force of laws; they neither oblige nor compel us to any course of action, but leave us at liberty; and if it be sometimes a duty and a mark of spirit to assert and defend them, it is often, also (I might say much oftener), a virtue and an evidence of magnanimity to waive them, and to forbear to insist on them.

That "all men are created equal" is, as our Declaration of Independence affirms, *a self-evident truth;* and therefore not to be understood in any other than a self-evident sense. All men have reasonable souls, capable of willing and thinking and of moral accountability; and their bodies are made out of the same dust, and are cast in the same mold. Compared with creatures below them, they have the same natural advantages; and compared with creatures above them in the scale of being, they have the same natural imperfections. Their natural wants and desires are the same; affecting present good not (like the brutes) for its own sake, but as an instrument to some other good beside and beyond it, and thus indicating a capacity for greater happiness than this world can furnish. All, too, stand in a common relation to God as their Maker, and the Giver and Preserver of their life; all are created in His image; all have the marvelous faculty of articulate speech; and all have one and the same law for their rule of action; the law, namely, of that reasonable nature which God has given them. Like the variegated grass, no two blades of which are exactly alike, while all have a general resemblance, so men, while distinguished from one another by infinite varieties of body and mind, are yet all of one and the same kind, and consequently equal in all the essential properties of their kind. The differences that exist among them are the results of accident or fortune, of their own acts or of the government of Divine Providence; but not of their creation. They are *created* equal, and in all the essentials of their nature they must forever remain equal.

In a word, men compared with creatures of other kinds are equal in the essential properties of their kind; but when compared with one another, and considered as male and female, adults and children, rich and poor, sound and maimed, ruler and subject, master and servant, etc., etc., they are infinitely unequal; every man being distinguished from every other by some personal characteristic of his own. Both truths are patent, both instructive. Our equality results from the constitution of our nature; our differences result from accident or fortune, from our own virtues or vices, or from the allotments of Providence: the one suggests mutual benevolence and respect, and, inspiring a fixed sense of human dignity, serves to allay the discontents and envies, and to guard against the undue elations and depressions of mind that are apt to be generated by the other.

From this equality of nature results an equality of rights. The Maker of mankind has given life to them all; He has granted the earth to all of them in common, and to each one of them in particular a property in his own person and labor; and He wills the happiness of them all. Hence all men have by nature an equal right to life, liberty, property, and the pursuit of happiness, subject only to the limitations of the law of Nature. The *natural rights* of man, therefore—those that arise from the law of Nature before the superinduction of any other law—are *equal.* For the very reason, however, that men are equal by nature, have the same wants and desires, affect the same things, and have equal natural rights, they are liable to jostle and interfere with one another, and to come into perpetual collisions, rendering their natural rights useless to many, and infinitely precarious to all. In order, therefore, to prevent feuds and dissensions, to provide for their mutual interests, and to enable them to exercise their rights in harmony, they define their relations, and their respective spheres of possession and action; and, to give permanence to these friendly and peaceable arrangements, they form compacts and institute governments. These compacts and governments, not contradicting the law of Nature (for in this case they are null and void), but being agreeable to it, are, when formed, bound upon the parties who form them by the law of Nature, which requires men to be faithful to their engagements; and bound also not only on the contracting parties, but, in many cases, on their families also, and their children that come after them. Now it is evident that these new laws and compacts restrain the former rights of men, and create new ones. Men surrender some of their rights for the sake of obtaining others, or they transfer their private rights to a public person, for the sake of promoting their mutual security and welfare. These concessions and transfers the law of Nature (while they conform to it) does not permit men to revoke, and hence Nature and Revelation require submission to the magistrate, while the magistrate enforces the observance of these laws and contracts. Natural right, therefore, is of no avail to justify the infraction of laws and contracts to which we have once consented. A man's natural right to dispose of his own person in marriage is no justification of bigamy after the law has tied him to one woman; nor will his natural right to come and go whithersoever he pleases and help himself to the fruits of the earth, clear him from the guilt or penalty of trespass if he enters his neighbor's field and reaps his corn against his will, and in violation of the law which protects him in his property. That cruelty and oppression may justify men, in extreme cases, in falling back on their natural rights, few will deny; but for fancied grievances and imaginary wrongs to disturb the just and peaceful relations and settled institutions of society is, by the consent of all, a crime that deserves the severest reprobation.

What has been said opens the way for a just apprehension of *liberty*, which I take to be a right to freedom as restrained and regulated by law. The natural liberty of mankind is a freedom limited only by the law of Nature; the civil or political liberty of a people is a freedom which is further limited by those human laws and forms of government to which they are rightfully and actually subject. Natural liberty is an immediate gift of God to men, being bestowed on them in virtue of that human nature in which they are created. Civil or political liberty is a mediate gift of God to men, being bestowed on them through the medium or intervention of those political institutions which He enables them to form by His wisdom, and to preserve by His providence.

There are other senses of the word *liberty*, to which I shall presently advert, but on which I forbear to dwell, because I consider them irrelevant to the matter in hand. But there is an abuse of the word which deserves to be noted and exposed. For by *liberty* men often mean a freedom to do as they list, without regard to what is good and just; to consult their own present pleasure, without regard to justice, the good of mankind, and their real and eternal good. If I should say that there was no such liberty, and that they who fancied they had it, were really slaves to their lusts and passions, and to the author and instigator of evil, I should affirm, indeed, that which is true, but which might not carry conviction to all. Suffice it, therefore, to say, what none, I hope, will deny, that there is no such liberty given by God to any man, in any conceivable relation, or under any possible circumstances. For suppose a man to be free from all subjection to civil society and human laws, still he is not at liberty to think and to act, as his fancy, or humor, or passion, may incline him. Even if all other laws are removed, he is always and everywhere subject to the law of Nature, and he is entitled to no other liberty, than a freedom to do that, and only that, which the law of Nature permits. Fancy and humor, instinct and passion, are not laws; they are only the workings and promptings of that lower and sensitive nature, which we have in common with the brutes; and they are to be restrained and regulated by the law of that reasonable nature, which constitutes our resemblance to our Maker. If men choose to call this state of lawlessness *liberty*, let them at least not degrade themselves and insult their Maker by calling it *natural liberty;* for natural liberty, or the liberty conferred on us by Nature, *i. e.*, by the God of Nature, is a freedom to do what the law of Nature enjoins, and only that which the law of Nature permits.

From liberty we naturally pass to the consideration of slavery, which is a privation of liberty in some sort and to some degree. But of what sort? and in what degree?

Men are apt to think that slavery is the opposite of liberty, and a privation of it; much the same as cold is the opposite of heat, and a privation of heat. Ask them what they mean by a slave, and the answer will probably be, that he is one who is deprived of his liberty; and, perhaps, after a moment's reflection, they will add, that he is deprived of it for no fault of his own.

But certainly there are many sorts of liberty with which slavery has no manner of connection, and which are common alike to the bond and the free.

Liberty sometimes denotes the power of choice and self-determination; the opposite of this liberty is not slavery, but necessity.

Sometimes liberty denotes the power to exercise reason and judgment in the direction of our conduct; the privation or destitution of this liberty is not slavery, but insanity or idiocy.

Liberty, again, sometimes denotes the power to think and act on our responsibility to our Maker. This is that sacred liberty of conscience, the attempt to coerce which, by intimidation and persecution, is accounted base by all generous minds. But this liberty is inalienable; no man, whether bond or free, can be deprived of it against his will; neither imprisonment nor death can extinguish it; for the man who is resolved on his integrity can not, as the poet tells us, be turned from his resolute purpose either by the barbarity of tyrants or the madness of the people.*

Liberty sometimes denotes the habit of virtue and rectitude. Thus we say, that "the service of God is perfect freedom," or liberty. The opposite of this liberty is habitual pravity, and is said to be slavery in a figurative sense, because its subject is under the dominion of his lusts and passions.

Liberty sometimes means the power to do this or that, and to move in one direction or another, accordingly as outward objects excite the appetites, or attract the senses of the body. This liberty belongs to brutes, and to man in virtue of that animal nature which he possesses in common with the brute creation. The mere privation of this liberty is not slavery; for men are deprived of it when they are imprisoned or manacled, but they are not therefore slaves. The order of human society deprives all its members of this liberty in some degree, without by any means reducing them to servitude.

* Justum et tenacem propositi virum
Non civium ardor prava jubentium,
Non vultus instantis tyranni
Mente quatit solida.

To liberty, in none of these senses, is slavery opposed. For slaves and masters are equally free, within their respective spheres, to choose and determine their own actions; to exercise the share of reason and judgment which God has given them; to follow the dictates of conscience; and to go hither and thither as they are moved by their senses, and external objects. All these senses of the word may, as already remarked, be discarded as irrelevant to the subject; nor can I conceive of any sort of liberty to which it can be reasonably pretended that slavery is opposed, unless it be bodily liberty, or civil liberty.

And here we come to the point at which the road divides, and the difference, indicated in our title-page, begins to appear. For it deserves to be carefully noted that the word *slavery* itself is taken in two senses, diametrically opposite: the one of which assigns to the slave a certain *status* in civil society, and, consequently, reserves to him his natural rights, and assigns to him only a limited subjection under the protection of the law; while the other puts him absolutely, and without reserve under the arbitrary dominion of his master. No wonder that men differ so radically on the subject of slavery, some denouncing it as abhorrent to nature, and a curse to humanity, others extolling it as a divine institution and a blessing, when they use the same *word* to represent things as wide asunder as the poles! Thus I find Mr. Locke* denying

* Works, Vol. II. p. 165, Fol. Ed.

that men, either among the Jews, or any other nation, ever sold themselves into slavery, and contending that it is against the law of Nature for a man to be a slave with his own consent. But what does Mr. Locke mean by slavery? He understands by a slave one who is subject "to the absolute and arbitrary power of another to take away his life when he pleases;" and he makes slavery to be "the state of war continued between a lawful conqueror and a captive." And in this sense all that Mr. Locke says about slavery is very true; but in *this sense* there is no such thing as a slave in the United States. If I turn to Johnson's Dictionary, I find that a slave is "one mancipated to a master; not a freeman; a dependent." Is slavery, in this sense of the word, contrary to the law of Nature, and were none sold to it among the Jews, or other nations; sold to be dependents and bondmen? We know the contrary, nor does Mr. Locke deny it; only he calls this state of servile dependence not *slavery*, but "*drudgery*." Thus we see that the same word is defined by standard authorities to mean things as different as light and darkness; the one making slavery to be a state of hostile oppression and subjection to *absolute* power, the other making it to be a state of peace and friendship, and of limited subjection in a well ordered society. How many strains of poetry, and bursts of oratory, and teachings of philosophy that have stirred our souls in childhood, and awakened our admiration in manhood, are suggested by the former sense!

And on the other hand, how many moving instances of attachment, fidelity, and bravery come to our remembrance, when we use the word in the latter sense! What man that lives, can regard slavery with any other sentiment than one of scorn and execration, if it mean what Mr. Locke and his followers understand it to mean? And, on the other hand, who can consider the ties that bind the slave (in the latter sense of the word) to his master, and the interest that he feels in all that concerns his master's family and estate, and not have kindly and generous sympathies excited in his bosom?

How far this equivocal meaning of the word *slavery* is the cause of the extreme and contradictory opinions that prevail on the subject, I leave to others to decide. That some grave conclusions, and of a very practical kind, are drawn from slavery in one of its aspects, and inadvertently applied to it in the other, I shall endeavor to show in another place. But for the present I am content to advertise the reader, that I consider the definition of slavery, as given by writers on the Civil Law, and adopted by popular writers on both sides of the Atlantic, to be inapplicable to the state of society in this country. For it is a fact, which, I suppose, will not be denied, that no one of the United States upholds that form of slavery which makes the slave the *absolute* property of the master. And if I am asked to state precisely what I mean by American slavery, I answer, that a slave is *a person who is related to society through another person, called a master, to whom he owes due service, or labor, for life, and from whom he is entitled to receive support and protection.*

This definition comprises, I believe, either expressly or by implication, all the essential characteristics of a slave, in that form of slavery which exists in our country.

1. It affirms that a slave is a person; and when it is added, that he is related to society through another person, it is implied that both are persons of the same nature, and possessed of the same natural rights, and owing reciprocally, the one to the other, all those human regards which are consistent with their relative positions.

2. It affirms that a slave is a person who holds not an immediate, but only a mediate * relation to the community in which he lives.

3. It affirms that a slave is a person who owes service or labor to another, called his master; in which is implied, that his labor is not his own, to dispose of as he pleases, but belongs to his master, to be disposed of as his master directs.

4. It affirms that the slave owes his labor to his master, not for a term of time, but for life; which implies, that the master has a right to, or property in. the slave's labor for life.

* For an explanation of these terms, see below, Chapter Fourth.

5. It affirms that the slave owes *due* labor to his master; by which I mean, that he owes it only in due measure, and in proportion to his abilities; and, consequently, that the master has the right to exact it only in the same measure; not to overwork his slave, but to require of him only such work as is reasonable.

6. When it is affirmed that the master has a right to the due labor of a slave for life, it is implied that he has the right, also, to transfer that right to others, under the same limitations, receiving an equivalent in return.

7. It is affirmed that the slave has a right to claim from his master support—food, clothing, shelter, in sickness and in health; and protection also from insult and violence.

These several particulars will be more fully explained in subsequent chapters. The form of slavery which they indicate, is *limited*, and not *absolute;* and I call it *American* slavery, because it is in fact the form, and the only form, in which slavery legally exists in any of the United States. It is this limited form of slavery which I purpose to defend; not by an appeal to *local* or *positive* law, whether State or Federal, but by an appeal to the LAW of NATURE, or the principles of universal justice.

CHAPTER III.

THE LAW OF NATURE, AND ITS RIGHTS.

HAVING defined slavery, and undertaken to compare it with the law of Nature, in order to ascertain its conformity or repugnance thereto, a due regard to method requires me to explain, more distinctly than I have hitherto done, what I mean by the law of Nature.

First, however, in order to allay the fears of those who think that all recognition of Natural Religion is derogatory to Revealed, it may be proper to remark, that the expression *law of Nature* is capable of a twofold sense. It may denote a law founded in nature, in the relations and fitness of things, and directive of the common good; or it may denote such discoveries of that law as have been made by human reason, in the unassisted use of its present faculties. The distinction is obvious; for the law may be founded in nature, and yet we, through the weakness of our faculties, or the neglect of our opportunities, may have failed, in a degree or wholly, to discover it: as we see in geometry, which contains numerous propositions capable of a rigid demonstration, while yet the generality of men know little more of it than its axioms. In the former sense, the law of Nature comprises all those duties which flow from the relations in which we stand to God and our fellow-creatures; while in the latter sense it denotes no more than those principles and rules of morality and religion, which we, in the unassisted use of our faculties, are able to discover.

To what extent human reason is able, in its present state, without the aid of Divine Revelation, to discover the law of Nature, is a question on which there is a wide diversity of opinion. Had men retained, and not abused, that gift of reason which God originally bestowed on them, they would, probably, be able to discover, without doubt or perplexity, all the duties they owe to God and their neighbor. But the history of men makes it pretty evident, that they have abused their reason, and that, in consequence of this abuse, they are unable to discover the will of their Maker with that ease and certainty, which were originally in their power. They can but spell out, as it were, with pains and labor, those immutable truths which reason, in its pure and unclouded state, could read plainly and without an effort. They confess, indeed, universally their subjection to a law of higher authority than human edicts, but they are perpetually liable to mistake, and misapply its requirements. Antigone spoke the voice of Nature when, scorning the prohibition of Creon, she refused to violate that *divine law unwritten, infallible, which is always living, and of which no man can say when it began to dawn :*

> 'Ουδὲ, σθένειν τοσοῦτον ᾠόμην τὰ σὰ
> κηρύγμαθ' ὥστ' ἄγραπτα κἀσφαλῆ θεῶν
> νόμιμα δύνασθαι θνητὸν ὄνθ' ὑπερδραμεῖν.
> οὐ γάρ τι νῦν γε κἀχθὲς, ἀλλ' ἀεί ποτε
> ζῇ ταῦτα, κοὐδεὶς οἶδεν εξ' ὅτου' φάνη :

albeit, guided rather by her feelings than by her reason, she was mistaken in thinking that this eternal law made the rites of sepulture necessary to the repose of the soul. All mankind acknowledge the first and elementary principles of this divine law, which, indeed, are so easily apprehended and universally promulged, that they are said to be *written in the hearts* of men. Some few of the ancient Heathen, assisted, doubtless, to some extent, by traditionary revelation, have given us very admirable discoveries of the same eternal law, in the shape of elaborate deductions from its principles ; while to the Holy Scriptures we are indebted for its most luminous, most concise, and only authoritative exposition. So that I may safely unite in an appeal to the law of Nature, understanding thereby a law founded in Nature, stable, eternal, and sufficiently known, especially by Christians, to answer the ends of a law, without concerning myself in the inquiry whether men owe their knowledge of it exclusively to Divine Revelation, or, in part, to the independent discoveries of their own reason.

With the same propriety, indeed, that we deny the objective reality of the law of Nature, we may deny the objective reality of all other things, and so involve ourselves in universal skepticism. True and false, sweet and bitter, order and disorder, proportion and disproportion, beauty and deformity, light and darkness, are differences founded in nature, and not merely ideas existing in our minds. That the whole is greater than a part, that 2 is to 4 as 4 to 8, that a parallelogram is double a triangle on the same base and between the same parallels, are immutable truths, founded in the nature of things, independently of our perception of them. Light and darkness do not depend for existence on a man's eye, nor beauty and deformity on his taste, nor sweet and bitter on his palate; but they are real differences, founded in nature, and upheld by its immutable laws. It is the same in morals and religion. The nature of things, and the relations which they hold to one another, are such, that some habits and actions are agreeable to our reasonable nature and conducive to the common good, while others are repugnant to our reasonable nature, and detrimental to the common good. It is evidently the design of Nature and the will of its Author, that we should choose and practise the one class of habits and actions, and avoid the other; and this will of the Author of Nature, so far as it is discoverable by us, is to us a law; a law laid in Nature, and always binding on men, unless the Author of Nature see fit, for great and wise ends, to dispense with it, and to prescribe actions (as, for example, Abraham's sacrifice of his son), which, if the law were not dispensed with by its supreme Author, would be an infraction of it.

Those actions which are agreeable to the law of Nature, which are due to others by the relations in which we stand to them, and are conducive to the common good (and the *common good*, be it observed, includes the honor of God, as well as the happiness of men), are said to be right, virtuous, and dutiful; *right*, as being done according to that *straight rule* which is the shortest way to happiness; *virtuous*, as being eminently worthy of (*vir.*) *man*, who is made in the image of his Maker; and *dutiful*, as being *due* to our Creator and our fellow-creatures, in virtue of the relations we hold to them. Actions opposite to these are wrong or crooked, vicious, and undutiful. And we might as well say that proportion and disproportion are created by the rules of mathematics, the beautiful and deformed by canons of criticism, light and darkness by the principles of natural philosophy, or true and false by the *ipse dixit* of the metaphysician, as to say that right and wrong, virtue and vice, are the mere creation of human law. Evidently the distinction in the case last mentioned, as well as in the others, is prior to the decrees and enactments of human legislators; prior even to the written revelations of the Almighty; founded in, and equally immutable with, the very nature of things: and the immutable rule which distinguishes what is essentially right from what is essentially wrong, is called the law of Nature; not as if Nature had no other laws, for, undoubtedly, the investigations of natural science, and taste, and all the other branches of human philosophy, presuppose certain laws of Nature to which they respectively refer; but, by way of eminence, and because of all the laws founded in Nature that which distinguishes right from wrong, and defines those actions which are consonant to universal reason, and promotive of universal happiness, is adapted, on this earth, only to the human nature, and is incomparably the most worthy of human consideration and study.

To discover and interpret this divine law, and apply it to the regulation of human conduct, is the province of reason. In matters of taste, the final appeal is to our *feelings*. We can give no other explanation of beauty and deformity in nature, than to say that the one excites within us pleasant, and the other unpleasant emotions. We consult the feelings of men as they are affected agreeably or otherwise, by outward objects, and from the facts thus collected we form canons of criticism, and establish, approximately at least, a standard of taste. But right and wrong are matters of reason, and not matters of taste; and though we speak of the beautiful and deformed, the lovely and the unlovely, in morals and religion, yet what we mean is, if we would talk sense, not what is in the first instance agreeable or disagreeable to our feelings, but what is agreeable or disagreeable to the relations in which we stand to God and our fellow-creatures (which is a matter for reason to decide), and to our feelings accordingly as they are or are not trained to a just perception and appreciation of these relations. In inquiries of this sort, therefore, feeling is to be discarded as a final arbiter. For feeling can not explain law, nor tell us what it prescribes, or what it forbids; and no more can it comprehend the relations of man to the universe, and define the actions which are congruous or incongruous to these relations. Feeling can not inform us what actions are most productive of good, or what of evil, to mankind at large, or to any individual among them. The investigation of human duty, under any of these formulas, namely, what is right or wrong, becoming or unbecoming, good or evil, is exclusively the province of reason. In inquiries of this nature, feeling, even were men pure and perfect, would be of no avail; and taking men as they are, corrupt and imperfect, it is easy to see that it may become a fallacious and ruinous guide. In ascertaining the law of Nature, therefore, on any given subject, let us aim in the first place to be guided by reason; and to consider actions as right or wrong, just or unjust, good or evil, not by the feelings which they excite, but by the feelings they ought to excite, and by their agreement or disagreement with those principles and rules of moral conduct which approve themselves to the reason of mankind.*

If it be said that every man must look for this divine law to the promptings of his own conscience, I answer that conscience is indeed the vicegerent of God in the soul; but then I must contend that conscience is neither feeling nor instinct, but that it is simply the reason or understanding itself applying its light to the government of its own moral actions. But this light or knowledge by which the conscience proceeds is capable of being reduced to distinct propositions; and accordingly as these propositions are true or false, accordingly as they do or do not declare the immutable law which Nature prescribes, the conscience which adheres to them and follows them, directs us either right or wrong, and leads us either to good or to evil.

As those propositions which determine, or ought to determine, the conscience, relate to the moral conduct of men, and are designed to show us the consequences of our moral actions, they are called *practical*, to distinguish them from others of a *theoretical* or *speculative* kind. And for the same reason that those precepts,

* The origin and causes of the habit, now so common, of appealing to the feelings for the arbitration of grave questions in morals and religion, would form a curious subject of inquiry. The habit is very flattering to indolence and self-conceit; and has, perhaps, been fostered by the word *heart* in our English Bibles; which in our language denotes the *feelings* or *affections*, but which in the Hebrew, and also in the New Testament Greek, comprises the *understanding* and *judgment* as well as the affections.

which are designed for the regulation of the conscience, are called *practical dictates*, the conscience itself is commonly called by our older writers the *practical reason*, or the *practical understanding.* The terms are, indeed, scholastic, and have now become obsolete; but it is much to be feared that the disuse of them has helped to blind the public mind to the true nature and office of conscience, and to propagate the delusion which makes *conscience* another name for *self-will.*

The dictates of conscience, therefore, in the proper sense of the words, are the deductions which reason makes, or is capable of making, or the discoveries which, when made, she acknowledges to be true, of the everlasting law of Nature. Those dictates assume different forms corresponding to the methods in which reason proceeds. For sometimes we proceed in the analytic method; and assuming that nature intends the *common good*, that is to say, the honor and glory of the Creator and the welfare of the creature, and seeing that of all possible actions some one tends more than others to promote this end, we infer that this action is *best* to be done. Or, proceeding in the synthetic way, we prove that some actions are suited to our reasonable and social nature, and to the relations in which we are placed to God and our fellow-creatures, and that others are unsuited; and thence argue that the former are fit and ought to be done, and that the latter are unfit and ought not to be done. Moreover, regarding the good and evil consequences of our actions as the *sanctions* annexed by Nature to the rule which she prescribes, and as imparting to it the force of a *law*, reason, in the name of God, lays on herself the obligation to do those things which are agreeable to the rule, and to avoid the contrary, and thus delivers her dictates in the form of commands. But, whichsoever of these forms be adopted, the result is the same; for whether my reason judges a thing to be *best*, or tells me that I *ought* to do it, or *commands* me to do it, I am equally obliged to do it.*

Proceeding in one or other of these methods, reason discovers to us, and devolves upon us, our obligation to practise those primary duties which we owe to God, to ourselves and our fellow-creatures; such as piety to God and benevolence to men, sobriety and chastity, prudence and constancy, moderation and equity, fidelity and gratitude, innocence and rectitude, candor and honesty, and in general all those virtues which are suited to our reasonable and sociable nature, and to the relations and circumstances in which we are placed, and which promote the honor of God and the good of men, and form us to the habits of self-control. From the obligation of these virtues are deduced those precepts which enjoin us to love and reverence our Maker, to be grateful to parents and benefactors, to do no harm to the innocent, to be faithful in our observance of compacts, and others of

* See Cumberland's Laws of Nature, c. 4.

a similar nature. These virtues, indeed, have been taught, and these precepts delivered in the Holy Scriptures with wonderful plainness and with divine authority. But they are not original with the Scriptures. The Ten Commandments, which are a digest of them made by the finger of God, were no *new* law at the time they were delivered, but *declarative** of that eternal law which dawned forth in the creation; a law founded not in the opinions of men, but in the reason and nature of things; engraven, as it were, on the heart of every man; confessed by all nations, and contradicted by none; and expressed with great clearness and force by some Heathen moralists as well as by Christian divines. This is that LAW OF NATURE which is of higher origin than human authority, and unalterable by senate or people. For, as Cicero admirably argues, if the laws of the people, and the decrees of princes, are *constitutive*, and not merely *declarative*, of right and justice, then robbery, adultery, and forgery would be right and virtuous, if once they were enacted by the decrees and ordinances of the multitude; and if, as with bitter irony he adds, there be such rare virtue in the suffrages of fools as to change the nature of things, why do they not ordain by their votes that poison be accounted healthy food? and if their

* The only exception is in relation to a part of the fourth commandment, which is *declarative* of the law of Nature, in so far as it requires us to set apart a portion of our time to the service of religion, but *positive* and *arbitrary* in so far as it *specifies* that portion, and makes it to be every *seventh* day.

laws can make right out of wrong, why can not they make those things preserve life, which naturally destroy it? *

From the law of Nature spring the rights of Nature; which, as already intimated, are of two kinds. The first kind comprises those rights which consist in a liberty to exact of others, what the law of Nature requires them to render to us; and the second comprises those rights which authorize us to have, or to do, all that the law of Nature does not forbid.

Of the former kind there are evidently two sorts which, for the sake of distinction, we may call direct and indirect. The former is created by the direct constitution of Nature, and without the intervention of any act on the part of the person, from whom obedience is exacted, to authorize this exaction; as, for example, the

* Quod si populorum jussis, si principum decretis, si sententiis judicum, jura constituerentur; jus esset latrocinari; jus, adulterare; jus testamenta falsa supponere, si hæc suffragiis, aut scitis multitudinis probarentur. Quæ si tanta potestas est stultorum sententiis atque jussis, ut eorum suffragiis rerum natura vertatur; cur non sanciunt, ut quæ mala perniciosaque sunt, habeantur pro bonis ac salutaribus? aut cur, cum jus ex injuria lex facere possit, bonum eadem facere non possit ex malo? And he adds, that a good law is distinguished from a bad by no other rule than that of nature; and that the distinction not only of right and wrong, but of all virtues and vices, is in like manner founded in nature. Atqui nos legem bonam a malâ nullâ aliâ nisi naturæ normâ dividere possumus. Nec solum jus et injuria a naturâ dijudicantur, sed omnino omnia honesta ac turpia, nam et communis intelligentia nobis notas res efficit, easque in animis nostris inchoavit, ut honesta in virtute ponantur, in vitiis turpia.—*De Legibus*, lib. 1, sect. 16.

right of parents over their children. Rights of the latter sort presuppose the intervention of such an act, and may therefore be said to be *indirectly* created. For example: the law of Nature (and not *only* the law of the land) gives the supreme magistrate, in every settled commonwealth, a right to exact obedience of the subject; but then it supposes the previous *consent* of the subject, either expressed or implied, to the magistrate's authority. In this case, the right of the magistrate may be called a *natural* right, inasmuch as it is created by natural law; but the right is evidently of a different sort from one which would give the magistrate liberty to exact obedience without the subject's consent.

Of the former sort of rights, or those which grow out of the direct constitution of nature, I am not aware that there is any variety. Nature gives the parent a right to exact obedience from his child; but besides this, I know of no instance in which Nature gives one man a direct right to exercise dominion over another. Even the right of the husband over the wife is not *directly* bestowed on him by Nature, but is obtained in the first instance by the consent of the woman or of her parents. And so, in all cases, that of parents alone excepted, the right of dominion, when bestowed by the law of Nature, is bestowed only in virtue of some act, expressed or implied, on the part of the subject to justify it; whence it is, I suppose, that we have in the Decalogue, which is declarative of the law of Nature, an *express* command to *honor father and mother*, but no *express* command to defer to any other human authority; the obligation to obey the magistrate, and others invested with lawful authority over us, being enjoined only by *implication*, and in consequence of that *analogy* which other lawful authority bears to the parental.

Natural rights of the other kind, or such as consist in a liberty to have, or to do, what the law of Nature does not forbid, are numerous. The chief of them are, a right to self-preservation; a right to life and limb and the products of our labor; a right to personal liberty, and a right to the pursuit of happiness.

It should be well observed, however, that the rights of Nature are necessarily limited by the law of Nature. For right, being a liberty to have or to do what the law permits, perishes and becomes extinct directly it leads us to do what the law forbids. The *rights* of Nature, therefore, are a nullity, the moment they are exercised in violation of the *law* of Nature; inasmuch as their very essence consists in a liberty to do that, and only that, which is consistent with the law of Nature.

Of the limitation of rights of the former kind, or those which entitle us to exact what is due to us from others, I shall have occasion to speak in a future chapter; and shall conclude the present chapter with a brief review of rights of the latter kind. And, first, of the right of self-preservation.

Hobbes, who has been more successful in poisoning

the mind of Great Britain (and, consequently, of this country) with infidel error than have all her clergy in imbuing it with Christian doctrine (for a fool or a madman may destroy in a day more than a hundred skillful architects can build up in a year); Hobbes, I say, opens the fourteenth chapter of his Leviathan, by telling us that "The right of nature, which writers commonly call *Jus Naturale*, is the liberty each man hath to use his own power for the preservation of his own nature; that is to say, of his own life; and, consequently, of doing any thing which, in his own judgment and reason, he shall conceive to be the aptest means thereunto." Hence, I suppose, the maxim, which is now-a-days in every body's mouth, that "Self-preservation (meaning thereby the preservation of one's *bodily* life) is the first law of nature." One is ashamed to think that such a maxim can have currency in a Christian country, when the very heathen have taught us, both by doctrine and illustrious examples, that it is better to die virtuously than to live dishonorably. I shall not stop to refute the fallacies of Hobbes, but shall merely affirm, what I am sure none but an atheist will deny, that no man has an *absolute* right to preserve his own life, but that every man holds the right under these two limitations; first, that if religion or the public welfare demand it, he is ready to part with it: and, second, that in preserving his own life, he will do wrong to no innocent person. For, as Bishop Lucy eloquently says (*Obser. on Lev.*, p. 167; London,

A. D. 1663): "To live only, is to be a *beast*, a *plant* only; but to live virtuously and reasonably, to glorify that God who gave him those abilities by which his life is happy, that is the end of man, and of man's *life;* which he is to leave then, when he can not enjoy it upon these conditions; and to a Christian man, as to the best of philosophers who had thoughts and assurance of eternity, this *life* hath been reputed of little value, and to die, no misery; because it is but the passage to a better and more spiritual *life*, although perhaps there may be some difficulties in opening the gate."

The same, *mutatis mutandis*, may be said of the other rights of Nature. They are none of them *absolute*, but are all *limited* by that law of Nature which creates them. They, therefore, vanish and expire the instant they are exerted in violation of the obligation which is imposed on every man to promote the common good; in other words, to live for God, and for his fellow-creatures, and for life eternal. It is the foulest of moral leprosy to assert these rights in defiance of the law which creates them. Men have the right to life and limb, and the products of their own labor, the right to preserve their liberty, the right to pursue their happiness, not *as they please*, but only under the restraints of that Eternal Law which commands them to keep compacts inviolate, to do no harm to the innocent, and, in a word, to fulfill the dictates of universal justice. To vindicate natural rights, therefore (supposing them to be infringed), or to encourage others to vindicate them, by means of theft, robbery, and murder, is, indeed, in all righteous judgment, "to sow the wind, and reap the whirlwind;" for rights, so vindicated, vanish, and only the guilt remains of having violated the Eternal Law which created them.

P. S. The following descriptions or definitions of the law of Nature are principally taken from authors who have treated *professedly* on the subject. These authors, though two of them were civilians, were all eminent in Christian theology; and hence they must have thought that not only the Decalogue, but also the precepts of our Blessed Lord and His Apostles, except so far as they relate to *external* religion, are declarative of a *prior* law inlaid in Nature by its divine Author.

"The law of Nature," says Dr. Jortin, "is the primary and original law of God, the eternal and unchangeable law of morality, which necessarily arises from the nature of rational creatures, and from their relation to God and to each other. And so the wisdom of this law is the very same as the wisdom of God's creation itself. For God hath so made us, that, if we would behave ourselves towards one another, according to our power and abilities, according to the best of our judgment, to the dictates of sober reason, and the suggestions of conscience, universal harmony and all its blessed effects would ensue." *

* Sermons, vol. v., p. 421.

"Since it is inconsistent with the nature and condition of man," says Puffendorf, "that he should live entirely loose from all law, and perform his actions by a wild and wandering impulse, without regard to any standard or measure; it follows that we make inquiry into that most general and universal rule of human action, to which every man is obliged to conform, as he is a reasonable creature. To this rule custom hath given the name of *Natural Law*, and we may call it likewise the law *universal* and *perpetual;* the former in regard that it binds the whole body of human race, the latter, because it is not subject to change, which is the disadvantage of *positive* laws." *

Grotius comes nearer to a definition: "Natural law," he says, "is the rule and dictate of right reason, showing the moral deformity, or moral necessity, there is in any act, according to its suitableness or unsuitableness to our reasonable and social nature; and, consequently, that such act is either forbidden or commanded by God, the Author of Nature." †

Bishop Cumberland's definition is more profound and rigid: it includes in it not only *precept*, but *promulgation* and *sanction*, and thus comes fully up to the requisitions of a *law*. "The law of Nature," he says, "is a proposition, proposed to the observation of, or impressed upon, the mind, with sufficient clearness, by the

* Law of Nature and Nations, book ii., c. 3, sect. 1.

† Gro. De Jur. Bel. et Pacis, lib. i., cap. 1, s. 10.

nature of things, from the will of the First Cause, which points out that possible action of a rational agent, which will chiefly promote the common good, and by which only the entire happiness of particular persons can be obtained."

To which I may add, as expressive of the *matter* of the law, the following quotation from Bishop Butler's dissertation "Of the Nature of Virtue":

"As much as it has been disputed wherein virtue consists, or whatever ground of doubt there may be about particulars, yet in general there is in reality an universally acknowledged STANDARD of it. It is that which all ages and all countries have made profession of in public; it is that which every man you meet puts on the show of; it is that which the primary and fundamental laws of all civil constitutions, over the face of the earth, make it their business and endeavor to enforce the practice of upon mankind; viz., justice, veracity and regard to the common good."

CHAPTER IV.

GENERAL DIVISIONS OF SOCIETY.

In all human society, and under every form of government, we find two general divisions of persons; the one holding an *immediate*, the other a *mediate* relation to the community in which they live. It is competent to persons of the former description to dispose of themselves and their affairs as they please, with no other limitation than that which is laid on them by the laws of the community to which they belong. They may follow what trade soever or profession they choose; they may hold property and form engagements in their own name and right; they may squander their estate, and reduce themselves to poverty and vagrancy; or they may deprive themselves for a time of their bodily liberty, and for the sake of avoiding the evils of penury and vagrancy, and of getting an honest livelihood, they may subject themselves to the dominion of another, by binding themselves out to service, or enlisting in the army or navy, if they happen to live in countries in which armies and navies are maintained. This division of persons comprehends, in most countries, the great bulk of the inhabitants, artisans, lawyers, soldiers, physicians, merchants, tradesmen, laborers, etc., etc., who have attained to what is called their majority; or who, in other words, have reached a certain age (which in our country and Great Britain is twenty-one, in France twenty-five, in Holland thirty), which is prescribed by the State in order to their admission to the rights of citizens.

But, besides these persons, there have always been, under every form of government, from the most stringent despotism to the purest democracy, a large number of persons who stand only in a *mediate* relation to society, or to its governing power; or who, in other words, are related to it through the medium of others. In every civilized country all persons, who have not attained their majority, are of this description; to a certain extent, also, all married women, without regard to age, are of this description; and in many ages and countries, the relations of master and servant have been such, that servants have been all their life long persons of the same description. Minors, for instance, however well qualified to transact business for themselves, are related to society only through their fathers or guardians; wives through their husbands; and servants (except those who are citizens) through their masters. The relation of this whole description of persons to the society in which, or to the government under which, they live, is such that they are incapable of direct communication with it, and enjoy its benefits, and receive its protection only through the medium of others. This distinction of persons into those who act in their own right, and those who act only in the right of another, is fundamental; and having obtained under all governments, must be confessed to be founded in Nature, and a necessary element of social order.

The foundation of this distinction I take to be this, viz., that States, or communities of men, were originally formed by fathers of families; and that the theory on which they were founded, and are still administered and conducted, supposes their power to be lodged in the men of which they are composed, not simply as they are persons, but as they are, or are capable of becoming, fathers of families. The family was in order of time before the State, and the State is a combination of fathers and masters for the better protection of themselves and their families. Reason points to this as the probable origin of political communities, and history attests the fact of such origin. Men's reverence for the law of Nature is not, as a general rule, strong enough to enable families to live together in safety and peaceable communion under that law alone, and without the intervention of civil government to coerce the unruly to its observance. Lust, avarice, and ambition, with their abominable progeny of violence, fraud and rapine, bring dismay and desolation on families; and the state or political community is simply a contrivance, by which the heads and natural protectors of families shall be able to concentrate their will and strength in laws and forms of judicature to ward off from them disgrace and ruin. Hence the reasonableness and necessity of the provision, not otherwise to be explained or justified, which excludes the larger numerical portion of every political community from a direct participation in its control. The right of suffrage is then truly universal when it is extended to all the adult males of the State, without regard to distinctions of property; it can not go beyond this limit, and be extended to women, without violating the main principle on which the very being of the State rests for support, which is the subordination of wives to their husbands, of children to their fathers, and of slaves (in every community which has them) to their masters. Women are cared for and protected in their natural rights by the State, and so are children, and so are slaves in those countries in which they chance to form one of the classes of society; but women, children, and slaves are not the State, are not the protectors of society. Their position is one of subordination and dependence; and men—freemen—whether they be "the lords of creation" or not, are in fact the lords and rulers of the political community to which they belong.

And not only *in fact*, but *of right;* for a little reflection will convince us that Nature and right reason point to men as the proper depositories of political power, and restrain two, at least, of the classes above indicated to that mediate relation to the State which, in fact, they hold.

In the case of children, the wisdom and justice of the rule are apparent. Nature itself, while they are too weak to take care of themselves, has evidently entrusted them to the care of their parents; and to this end has implanted in the bosom of parents a strong affection for their offspring. But, in order to exercise this care over their children, to feed, clothe, and educate them, it is essentially necessary that their parents have the government of them. Nature, therefore, requires the subordination of children to their parents, and to the father rather than the mother (if the children are born in wedlock), as being the head of the wife, and consequently of the family. The State presumes this subordination; regards children as under the care of their parents, deals with them through their parents, and, in the case of the death of the parents, continues to govern them in the same indirect way through the medium of tutors or guardians.

The beneficence of this provision, and the true position of the State in relation to it, appear in another respect. Children, through weakness and inexperience, are not qualified to make engagements for their own benefit; their simplicity and ignorance would render them an easy prey to fraudulent and designing persons; and if they had the power to bind themselves by their own acts they would be soon involved in confusion and ruin. The law of Nature accounts them incapable of forming engagements to their own damage. They gain the necessary understanding and experience, which qualify them to form engagements and contracts, at different times of life, some at an earlier age, some at a later. It is impossible to make a particular rule for every one; and hence the State steps in and determines a particular moment when they shall all be accounted capable of acting in their own name and right. Thus the State is the minister of Nature, and gives force and effect to her intention. It acknowledges the paternal relation to be prior to its own relation; and its admission of the son to immediate relation with itself is simply the collective consent and concurrence of fathers to the point of time when their paternal authority shall be surrendered, and their sons admitted to a direct participation in the government, which they originally founded, and which they continue to direct.

Nor is this subjection of men to the authority of the State, during their minority, without any voice in its affairs, founded exclusively on the paternal right of government, but also on their own consent. "For it may fairly be presumed that if an infant, at the time of its birth, had the use of reason, and saw that its life could not be preserved without the care of the parents, to which must be joined a power over itself, it would readily consent to the same, and desire for itself a comfortable education from them."* Men, therefore, during their minority, are not deprived of their natural rights, but are, with their presumed consent, protected by their fathers in the enjoyment of those rights.

The fact that the State owes its origin to a union of families, explains and justifies also the relation in which women stand to it. For they were subordinate to their husbands before the State or political community existed; they became at first related to the state through their husbands; and the same reasons which led to the origin of this mediate relation serve to perpetuate it. They were not the framers of the body politic, and are not its administrators; because they were not, and are not, heads of families, but occupy in the family a subordinate position.

But what, it may be asked, is the ground and origin of the family relation? By what right does the husband exercise authority over his wife? On what ground is the father's authority over the children made superior to that of the mother? The life of the offspring is equally due to both parents; and Nature, by infusing into the bosom of the mother a stronger parental attachment, and annexing to her relation greater pains and sorrows, seems, on a superficial view, to give her a higher claim to their obedience. Why, then, is not the woman invested with the chief power over her children,

* Puffendorff's Whole Duty of Man, book ii., c. iii.

and made, instead of the man, the medium of deriving to them the protection and benefits conferred on them by the State?

The proximate solution of these questions is found, no doubt, in the institution of marriage. For if children are born out of wedlock, either actually, as sometimes happens in civil society, or hypothetically, as when we fancy men living in a state of nature; then the case would be otherwise: for children would then know no higher authority than that of the mother, and would owe subjection to her in preference to others.

But there is an answer to the question back of this: for marriage is not an expedient on which men have stumbled at random, nor a custom fastened on them by a senseless tradition; but it is *the* way indicated by Nature, and prescribed by Revelation, for the propagation of the human species. And marriage to every person who well considers it will appear to be not precisely a contract between equal parties, but a contract which takes its origin from the man, and in which mutual stipulations are exchanged, of comfort and protection on the one side, and of obedience and service on the other.

It is impossible for a sane man to believe that the mutual attraction of the sexes is mainly designed in the human kind, as among brutes, for the continuance of the species. No more revolting spectacle of brutality and misery can be imagined, than would be presented by the human kind, if it were propagated by casual and promiscuous intercourse. To suppose that God intended any such degradation of a higher species of His creatures to the level of a lower, is a virtual denial of His goodness and providence. Nature evidently teaches that the intercourse of the sexes among mankind is designed for higher ends than the propagation of the species, and that it ought to be regulated with a view to the care and education of children, and the orderly government of society. By infusing in the man a desire of offspring, and of filial affection and support, she points him to marriage as an indispensable means of fixing and ascertaining the paternal relation, which could not otherwise be known, and without the certainty of which, no man could know and love his children, and make their welfare the object of his study and labor. In this way Nature indicates the man as the proper party to propose and originate marriage. By endowing him also with the greater strength of body and mind (for though particular women may, and, doubtless, do excel particular men in both these respects, yet a comparison of the sexes on the whole leaves no reasonable doubt that the superiority belongs to the man), she unequivocally points him out as the head of the woman; and in so doing, she plainly designates the father as superior to the mother, in the rule and government of the family. Thus, if marriage requires the subordination of the wife to the husband, and gives the father a higher claim than the mother on the obedience of the children, it is no less evident that marriage itself, which involves these distinctions, is founded in nature; and that the preëminence of the man in the family was potentially wrought in human nature, before it was actually developed in the custom of nations, and prescribed by the Revealed Law. Man was created for society; society can not exist without government, nor government, unless there be one to rule, and others to obey; and He who created man, created in him, and with him, the rudiments of that government which is necessary for the simplest form of society. In the extension and enlargement of society, men are thrown more upon their own resources for the expedients of government; and in respect to these, God no otherwise ordains than as His overruling Providence directs. Families and tribes combine themselves into the nation under a single head, or they vest the supreme power in the hands of the few or the many; and hence the monarchy, hereditary or elective, the oligarchy, the democracy, etc., all which are the effects of human contrivance. But government, in its original or elementary form (which is patriarchal), is the more immediate operation of the Divine wisdom, and is stamped on Nature by the Divine decree. The man, from the necessity of Nature, and in obedience to her voice, becomes the founder of the family, and he chooses the woman to coöperate with him in the procreation and education of his children. He seeks, and receives her at her father's hands; and when he obtains her, he becomes to her what her father was before; her protector and guardian, her representative in society, and the person through whom she is related to the political body. To reverse this order, is to upheave the foundation of human society; and to approximate this reversal, and, under the specious pretext of bettering woman's condition, to work one change after another in her established relations with society, and to confer upon her one right after another inconsistent with these relations, is, by little and little, to disintegrate society, and to open the way for the ultimate reign of confusion and brutality. Women's rights are, with their own consent, secured to them through their husbands and fathers.

CHAPTER V.

RELATIONS TO THE STATE.

The power of the State, like all human power, is limited in its legitimate exercise by the law of Nature; and, if it contravene this law by acts that are unjust or oppressive, or rash and capricious, it imperils its own existence. Of flagrant violations of the law of Nature, there is little danger; an attempt to decree impiety to God, the contempt of parents, the perpetration of fraud, or any confessed immorality, would be rejected at once as suicidal and monstrous. It is only in the last stage of decay or the fullness of corruption that a political body can rush upon such manifest ruin. It is the hidden danger that is most to be dreaded. Rocks that tower in the air the ship of State easily avoids; but woe betide her when rocks that lie just beneath the surface of the waters are not laid down in the pilot's chart! And if the principles on which we have insisted, as developed in the formation and government of families, are really dictated by Nature; if they were in force antecedently to the constitution of the State, and underlie its existence, then every measure of legislation which tends to obliterate these principles, is as really, though less obviously, hostile to the true genius and welfare of the State as a statute would be which imposed virtue for vice, or vice for virtue. The State, no doubt, has the power to reduce the nonage of men below the limit which law and custom have prescribed, and to confer on women the civil rights and franchises which have been hitherto appropriated to men; but unless the power of the State in these particulars be exercised with discretion and with due regard to those principles which are the foundation of its own existence, there is manifest danger that it may counteract the design and law of Nature, and thus retrograde towards anarchy by means, perhaps, of those very measures which, as it fondly dreams, are to advance it in civilization and refinement.

A law of the State authorizing children to act in their own right at twelve or fourteen years of age, would be manifestly repugnant to Nature. It would be unjust, by depriving the parent of the right which Nature gives him to the child's subjection and service, and, by depriving the children of the correlative right to the parent's protection and care. It would be inexpedient, because it would confer the right of self-government on a large class of persons who are unfit for its exercise, and whose reckless improvidence would probably involve them in ruin. A law of the State declaring marriage to be merely a partnership or joint contract between two equal parties, would be also repugnant to Nature. It would sever in twain what Nature intends to be one; for man and woman, separately considered, are parts of one whole,* and it is only in their union that the human nature is entire. It would be unjust, by depriving the man of the subjection and service naturally due to him from the woman, and by depriving the woman of the comfort and protection which Nature gives her the right to claim from the man. It would be inexpedient, because it would subvert the foundation of that order which is essential to the peace and happiness of human society, and which Nature has laid in the physical and mental superiority of the man; and because by throwing uncertainty over the paternal relation, it would render men incapable of mutual confidence and alliance, of great and enduring works, of steady aim and purpose, and deprive them of their strongest motives to sober thought and persevering labor.

These principles, though questioned by some, are, on the whole, pretty firmly rooted in the human mind. It is almost universally admitted that the State is right in holding women and children to the full extent to which they are so held, in a *mediate* relation to itself; that the laws of the State which uphold this relation are de-

* "They twain," said GOD, at the beginning, "shall be ONE flesh." (Gen. ii. 24, comp. Mat. xix. 5.) The notion of Plato, that the humanity was originally one mass, and became male and female by separation, was probably not so much a sally of fancy, as a perversion of tradition.

clarative of the law of Nature as exhibited in the constitution of mankind; and that laws of an opposite design and tendency, by doing violence to Nature, would be productive of confusion and misery in human society.

But there is another class of persons among us, holding a mediate relation to the State, and that is persons who are bound to service for life, and who are related to the State only through those persons to whom they are bound. I say that there are such persons *among us;* for, believing that the States of the American confederacy are united in fact as well as in name, and that the Constitution which unites them is something more than a compact, I hope to be pardoned for regarding the people of the Southern States as in some real sense one with ourselves, and for looking upon their prosperity as our prosperity, and their institutions as our institutions. In this view, an inquiry into the moral quality and effect of a law, the aim of which would be to separate master and slave, and to bring slaves into immediate relation with the State, is so far from being a barren speculation that it is one in the solution of which all citizens of the United States may be expected to feel a deep and responsible interest.

But here we are in danger of being embarrassed by a verbal ambiguity. Men affix the same idea to the word *child;* but they affix, as already stated, various and discordant ideas to the word *slave.* And, by the way, it is worthy of remark, that a word which is used with so much latitude, and serves to cover such a variety of conditions, is utterly unfit to be used in an instrument that requires extraordinary precision of language; a fact that seems to have escaped the attention of those who deny that the Constitution of the United States recognizes *slavery* in any form, because it does not contain the word. *Bound to service*, which are the words of the Constitution, expresses one form of slavery, the recognition of which is entirely consistent with the rejection of slavery as the word is understood by Mr. Locke, Adam Smith, and other eminent authors. But of this more anon.

If slavery be a forced condition, upheld by the mere power of the strong over the weak; if it be an arbitrary deprivation of natural rights, tyrannical and cruel, unjust and oppressive; then, undoubtedly, a law of the State that should abolish it, would be so far from being repugnant to the law of Nature, that it would be imperatively demanded by it. For who doubts, or ever did doubt, that the law of Nature forbids injustice? He who contends that the State is bound to guard the natural rights of man, and to restrain, by the wisest and most effective measures in its power, tyranny and cruelty, oppression and injustice, may rely upon it that he shall not have me for an opponent. If slavery be, as its adversaries generally suppose, essentially unjust, it certainly needs no argument to show that justice requires its extinction, and it would only remain to devise those means for its extinction which prudence and wisdom would prescribe.

But what I hold and shall endeavor to show is, that slavery, considered as a settled institution of society, is not contrary to justice, nor an infraction of the natural rights of man. On the contrary, I suppose that the relation of master and slave, wherever it is duly established, is consonant to the law of Nature, binds both parties to reciprocal duties, and clearly conduces to their mutual welfare, and conduces also (though not always in the greatest degree), to the prosperity of the community.

Between the natural relations of the family, however, and those which are merely providential, there is this broad and ineffaceable difference, viz., that the former are not, and the latter are, dependent for their continuance on the will of the parties. While parent and child live, no power can annul the relation which Nature has created between them. The law of Nature, if Divine revelation be accepted as its interpreter, does not permit either husband or wife, separately or both together, under any circumstances or for whatever cause, to dissolve the bond that unites them; the parties may separate, but they can not free themselves from the bond; only the State, in virtue of the *limited* power which God has entrusted to it for the purpose, can release one of the parties from its obligations to the other. These natural relations, therefore, may be said to be ordinarily indissoluble. Not so, however, with that providential relation which subsists between master and slave, for the bond which unites them may be at any time dissolved by their mutual consent.

Hence it follows that the State has a much larger power over master and servant than it has over the other and more sacred relations of the family. It may annul the relation, with the express consent of the parties; it may presume on their consent, and extinguish the relation, when its extinction is manifestly conducive to the welfare of the parties immediately concerned, and demanded by high grounds of public expediency. It appears to me, however, that the authority of the State in this matter is by no means absolute. For when the relation is settled and the parties to it are, on the whole and in a reasonable degree, content with their respective stations, it is evident, I think, that a law of the State abolishing it would do violence to the law of Nature, and work manifold injustice and misery. For both masters and slaves have rights which the State is bound to respect: it has no right to deprive the master of that debt of service which the slave owes, without making him compensation: it has no right to deprive the slave of his master's care and protection, without putting him in a position in which he may earn his livelihood in health, and have a reasonable prospect (equivalent to what he had before) of support in sickness, decrepitude, and old age. Thus to deprive men of their social rights, and by a mere act of arbitrary power cancel obligations that are founded on eternal justice, is tyranny; and to do the same under the pretext of philanthropy and religion, is tyranny and hypocrisy combined. And if anything can add to the iniquity of such legislation, it is the fact that the rights and obligations thus trifled with are in order of Nature anterior to, and more sacred than, any which the State can create; for the relation of master and servant grows up in order of Nature next to that of parent and child, and the rights and obligations involved in it were of force before men formed themselves into political organizations. True, the State is supreme; it can not be called to account (though the men who govern it may be) for any of its acts; but as every violation of justice is followed by a righteous retribution of Providence, so the deprivation of slaves of the care and protection to which their servitude entitles them, has been found not only to involve them in ruin, but to inundate society with the evils of pauperism and vagrancy and an increase of crime.

But I find myself unconsciously anticipating the course of my argument, and assuming that the relation of master and slave is essentially just, and does no violence to natural rights. Let us look, then, to the origin and grounds of the relation; when we shall find, if I mistake not, that the position of the slave, though humble, is not dishonorable; unless, indeed, lowliness be accounted synonymous with meanness, and all servitude be branded as vile and reproachful.

CHAPTER VI.

THEORY OF SLAVERY.

"In the sweat of thy face shalt thou eat bread till thou return unto the ground," was part of the penalty which man incurred for his failure in that OBEDIENCE to the law of GOD, which had been made the condition of his continuance in the perfect knowledge and love of his Maker. It was not labor that constituted the penalty of his transgression, but the discomfitures and hardships that were thenceforward to be the accompaniments of labor. For, before the fall, "the Lord God took the man, and put him into the garden of Eden, *to dress it and to keep it*;" a plain proof, that as labor is one of the ends for which man's body was created, so was it also the condition on which he was to enjoy the products of the earth. Even in his state of innocence he was to till the ground; and if men had continued innocent, there seems no reason to doubt that, in process of time, the products of one country would have been exchanged for another, and that the auxiliary arts and sciences would have flourished in connection with agriculture and commerce. Labor which, under the blight of the fall, is irksome and oppressive, would have been, in a state of innocence, a delightful occupation; and the various connections and relations to which its manifold divisions and subdivisions naturally lead, would probably have been much the same as at present, only without that loathing and disgust, which grow out of a disordered body, and those turbulent outbreaks of oppression and cruelty, hatred and revenge, which are the bitter fruits of a disordered mind. The diversity of men's genius and talents, their various aptitude for all innocent pursuits and departments of industry, would have been as great as at present; for it is impossible to believe that integrity would have impaired their faculties, or restrained their development. In fact, we have only to see men as they are, and then, by an effort of imagination, to take away sin (and death, which is that method of departure from this world, which sin has introduced), in order to see what they would have been had they preserved their innocence.

But what (methinks, I hear the reader exclaim), do you think there could have been *bondage* in Paradise? Pray, why not? There are bonds of love and reverence, as well as bonds of fear and hatred and as it is the substitution of the love of self for the love of God and man, which makes bondage hateful, so we have only to drive out self-love, and to bring back the love of God and man in its place, in order to render bondage lovely and beautiful. In truth, dear reader, there has been no real bondage on this earth, unless it existed in Paradise; that wretched state, which the world calls bondage, being no more than a miserable and abortive experiment to effect, by power, a union, which is then only perfect when created by love.

I see no reason, then, why the relation of master and servant should not have existed in a state of innocence as well as that of husband and wife, parent and child. Certainly, the Christian religion, which assumes the fall of man as a fact, and aims to restore him to the state from which he has fallen, does not abrogate the relation of master and servant, but seeks to purge it of selfishness, and to reclaim it, as far as human infirmity allows, to a state of ideal perfection.

The state of servitude, as God designed it, and as it would have existed in Nature, had not Nature been vitiated by sin, and as it may still exist on earth, in proportion as men are redeemed from the curse by the grace of Christ, and realize the pattern which He prescribes, is eloquently described in one of the noblest chapters of that remarkable work of St. Augustine, "The City of God." The reader will find the passage suggestive of wholesome thoughts; and the old English version, made from that of Ludovicus Vives, is so redolent of antiquity, that I shall use it in preference to any modern and more polished translation. It is impossible to read it, and not feel that we are holding communion with the good father himself:

"Now God, our good Master, teaching us in the two chiefest precepts the love of Him and the love of our neighbor, to love three things, God, our neighbor, and ourselves, and seeing he that loveth God, offendeth not in loving himself; it followeth that he ought to counsel his neighbor to love God; and to provide for him in the love of God; since he is commanded to love him as his own self. So must he do for his wife, children, family, and all men besides: and wish likewise that his neighbor would do as much for him in his need: thus shall he be settled in peace and orderly concord with all the world. The order whereof is, first, to do no man hurt, and, secondly, to help all that he can. So that his own have the first place in his care; and those, his place and order in human society affordeth him more conveniency to benefit. Whereupon St. Paul saith, 'He that provideth not for his own, and, namely, for them that be of his household, denieth the faith and is worse than an infidel.' For this is the foundation of domestical peace, which is an orderly rule, and subjection on the part of the family, wherein the provisors are the commanders, as the husband over his wife, parents over their children, and masters over their servants: and they that are provided for, obey, as the wives do their husbands, children their parents, and servants their masters. But in the family of the faithful man, the heavenly pilgrim, there the commanders are, indeed, the servants of those they seem to command; ruling not in ambition, but being bound by careful duty; not in proud sovereignty, but in nourishing pity."

Beautiful ideal of human society when cemented by the love of God, "whose service," in whatever relation of life, "is perfect freedom." That servitude should be upheld by force, that the lords and tyrants of the people should affect to be their benefactors, is at once the offspring and penalty of the corruption of human society. "Ye shall not be so," said the divine Restorer; "but he that is greatest among you let him be as the younger; and he that is chief, as he that doth serve; * * I am among you as he that doth serve!" To reclaim man to his original state, not to increase the disintegration of society, by leavening it with the spirit of pride and rebellion, but to bind together husband and wife, parents and children, masters and servants, rulers and subjects, in the love of God, and in mutual and helpful dependence on one another for God's sake, is the design of "THE CITY OF GOD," the Church of the Redeemed; whose origin, history, and polity St. Augustine describes in the work I am quoting. The above extract was the conclusion of the chapter entitled, "Of the law of heaven and earth, which swayeth human society by counsel, and unto which counsel human society obeyeth." The next extract is the whole of the succeeding chapter, title and all:

"*Nature's freedom and bondage, caused by sin, in*

which man is a slave to his own affects (affections) though he be not bondman to any one besides.

"Thus hath Nature's order prescribed, and man by God was thus created. 'Let them rule,' saith He, 'over the fishes of the sea and the fowls of the air, and over everything that creepeth upon the earth.' He made him reasonable, and LORD only over the unreasonable; not over man, but over beasts. Whereupon the first holy men were rather shepherds than kings, God showing herein what both the order of creation desired and what the merit of sin exacted. For justly was the burden of servitude laid upon the back of transgression. And, therefore, in all the scriptures we never read *servant* until such time as that just man Noah laid it as a curse upon his offending son. So that it was guilt and not Nature that gave original unto that name. The Latin word *servus* had the first derivation from hence; that those that were taken in the wars, being in the hands of the conquerors to massacre or to preserve, if they saved them, then they were called *servi*, of *servo*, to serve. Nor was this effected beyond the desert of sin. For in the justest war, the sin upon one side causeth it, and if the victory fall to the wicked (as sometimes it may) it is God's decree to humble the conquered, either reforming their sins herein or punishing them. Witness that holy man of God, Daniel, who, being in captivity, confessed unto his Creator that his sins and the sins of the people were the real causes of that captivity.

"Sin, therefore, is the mother of servitude and first cause of man's subjection to man, which, notwithstanding, cometh not to pass but by the direction of the Highest, in whom is no injustice, and who alone knoweth best how to proportionate His punishment unto man's offences; and He himself saith, 'Whosoever committeth sin is the servant of sin;' and therefore many religious Christians are servants unto wicked masters, yet not unto freemen,* for that which a man is addicted unto, the same is he a slave unto. And it is a happier servitude to serve man than lust: for lust (to omit all the other affects) practiseth extreme tyranny upon the hearts of those that serve it, be it lust after sovereignty or fleshly lust. But in the peaceful orders of States, wherein one man is under another, as humility doth benefit the servant, so doth pride endamage the superior. But take a man as God created him at first, and so he is neither slave to man nor to sin. But penal servitude had the institution from that law which commandeth the conservation and forbiddeth the disturbance of Nature's order; for if that law had not been transgressed, penal servitude had never been enjoined.

"Therefore the apostle warneth servants to obey their masters and to serve them with cheerfulness and good-will; to the end, that if they can not be made free by their masters, they (may) make their servitude a free-

* "Their masters being slaves to their own passions, which are worse masters than men can be."—L. VIVES.

dom to themselves by serving them, not in deceitful fear but in faithful love, until iniquity be overpassed and all man's power and principality disannulled, and God only be all in all."*

In this admirable passage the theory of servitude is luminously developed. The relation of master and servant grows out of the wants of man, and is part of Nature's order; it is productive of no hardship, and is accompanied with no disgrace, but is alike beneficial and honorable. But the abuse of man's free will, which has disturbed the order of Nature, and brought degradation and misery in various degrees, on all the natural and instituted relations of human society, has blighted the relation of master and servant, rendering masters imperious and servants turbulent, and has thus caused the relation to be upheld by force, even in cases in which it ought to be upheld by charity. Christianity, which proceeds from the Author of Nature, can not violate the order of Nature. She takes Nature as her foundation, and builds on it a new superstructure, or repairs the ruins of the old. She does not destroy the man, but renews him; she does not annihilate the powers and faculties of the human mind, but gives them a new bent and superinduces on them the new habits of faith and charity. She does not abolish the natural relations of mankind, but breathes into them a new SPIRIT—the

* ST. AUGUSTINE'S "CITY OF GOD," *with the learned comments of Jo. Lod. Vives. Englished by J. A.* A. D. 1610. Bk. xix., c. 15.

love of God and man—and aims, by the energy of this HOLY SPIRIT, to restore them, as far as human infirmity allows, to what Christians, instructed in the oracles of God, believe to be their original, and what all others may perceive to be their ideal, perfection. And it is by the consistent application of the same principle—the reformation and conservation of human society, and not its destruction and disintegration, that Christianity is led, not to abrogate the relation of master and servant, but to restore it to its primitive innocence by an infusion of charity for the performance of its reciprocal duties, and of patience for the endurance of those evils which are at first the fruits, and are then made by God's just ordinance, the punishment of man's disturbance of the order of Nature.

All this, I confess, proceeds on the assumption that slavery, or servitude for life, does no violence to Nature, but is good and agreeable to Nature. For it is only that which is good that can be abused by man's perversity, and reformed from abuse by his renovation; since evil can neither be abused nor reformed, but is only fit to be restrained and abolished. This, then, is the next point we are to consider, and it will lead us to investigate the origin and essence of slavery, and the grounds on which it rests. Whence came it? what is it? and what are the reasons for its continuance? The investigation of these matters will form the subject of the following chapter.

CHAPTER VII.

ORIGIN AND NATURE OF SLAVERY.

THE father, not less by the voice of Nature, than by the appointment of God, is the head of his family. He was born, not for himself alone, but for his wife, his children, and all others whom he loves and is bound to protect. For the purpose of discharging these functions, he calls in the aid, and avails himself of the strength, the speed, or any other perfection of those animals that Nature has strewed around him, and intended for his assistance. In process of time arts are cultivated, and property is more unequably distributed. The wants of the rich are multiplied, and the poor are reduced to the necessity of bartering their labor for their sustenance. Hence the relation of master and servant; the one engaging to administer food and raiment, shelter and protection, and the other to undertake all proper labors and reasonable employments, as their own functions and abilities, and their master's wants and services should require.*

The relation, at first probably temporary, and as occa-

* See Dr. John Taylor's *Elements of Civil Law*, p. 410.

sion required, soon became permanent. "In the early ages of the world," says Puffendorff, "when men began to quit their primitive plainness and simplicity, to cultivate the method of living, and to enlarge their fortunes and possessions, it is very likely the wiser and richer sort invited those of less parts and less wealth to assist them in their business, for hire. Afterwards, when both parties found their benefit in this way of proceeding, the meaner tribe were by degrees persuaded to join themselves perpetual members to the families of the greater; under these conditions, that the latter should engage to supply food and all conveniences of living, and the former should bind themselves to undertake all proper labors and employments as their masters should direct. So that the first rise of servitude is owing to the voluntary consent of the poorer and more helpless persons, and is founded on that common form of contract *Do ut facias;* I promise to give you constant sustenance, upon condition that you assist me with your constant work."*

Besides this honest and natural desire of obtaining a livelihood, the passions and vices of men, and sometimes higher and more generous motives, have led them voluntarily to reduce themselves to servitude. The Hebrews (and I suppose Moses understood human rights) not only made slaves of foreign nations by conquest, but permitted slavery among themselves, and over their own people, for

* Law of Nature and Nations, Bk. VI., ch. iii., sec. 4.

the relief of extreme poverty, and for the payment of debts, as well as for the punishment of crime. The statement of Tacitus in regard to the Germans, is well known. In their passion for gambling, they used; when they had lost all else, to stake their liberty on the cast of a die; and he that lost voluntarily became a slave to the winner. An ancient Greek author, quoted by Grotius, speaks of thousands who are free, and who yet oblige themselves by contract to become slaves. So strongly, indeed, has this inclination at times prevailed among men, that in several countries it has been found necessary to restrain it by law. The practice was forbidden by the Egyptians, and consequently must have prevailed among them before it was forbidden. It was permitted in Athens, until the time of Solon; one of whose laws, as we learn from Plutarch, enacted *σώμασι μὴ δανέιζεσθαι*, that men should not borrow money on their bodies. "Among the Romans, it was a known trick with sharpers, to suffer themselves to be sold for the sake of going shares in the price: and for their punishment, they were condemned to real servitude." The practice was forbidden by the Petilian law.* In view of these facts, it may be questioned whether slavery be indeed (as is commonly supposed) the creature of *local law*, or whether men have not the right universally to

* See Grotius, Bk. II., ch. xxv. sec. 27, and the notes; and Puff. Bk. VI., ch. iii, sec. 7.

dispose of themselves and their services for life, except so far as they are restrained from doing so by the law of the place or country in which they reside.

However this be, it is by no means certain that servitude had its origin exclusively in war. In the judgment of the eminent authors whom we have quoted, it was originally founded on contract; and the relation of master and servant is probably more ancient than any other relation (that of husband and wife excepted) which is founded on contract. It dates back to a period anterior to the records of profane history, and may be shown to have existed in the family, before families were grouped into nations, and to have involved rights which were not forfeited, but were recognized and respected under the more extended governments to which, in course of time, families were subjected.

The lawyers, indeed, would have us believe that servants owe their name, as well as their origin, to the fortunes of war: "*Servorum appellatio ex eo fluxit,*" say the digests, "*quod imperatores nostri captivos vendere, ac per hoc servare, nec occidere solent;*" but the lawyers are no authority in a question of etymology; not to add that servants were held as property before Roman generals made captives, or Rome herself had a being. The grammarians speak more to the point when they derive *servus* from the obsolete ἕρος *a servant* the aspirate being expressed by the letter *s* and the digamma of the Æolics by the letter *v*, which gives us *servos* from ἑρος just as *sylva* is derived from ὑλη, not to mention many other instances of the same kind. No doubt the condition of servitude was modified by war; of that presently; but first having traced it to its origin, let us observe its agreement with justice and equity.

Grotius distinguishes servitude into *perfect* and *imperfect*, meaning by the latter that kind of servitude which is for a term of time, or on certain conditions, the result of agreement or of positive law. Of the former he says:

"Perfect servitude is that which obliges a man to work all his life long for diet and other common necessaries, which, if it be concluded on natural terms, has nothing too hard and severe in it, for the perpetual obligation to service on the one hand is compensated by the perpetual certainty of being provided for on the other. They who let themselves out for daily labor often have not this assurance of being provided for, whence that which Eubulus has mentioned frequently happens

Εθελει δ'ανευ μισθου, etc.

'He was willing to stay with them for his victuals without wages.' The same comedian, in another place,

Πολλοι φυγοντες, etc.

'Many who have run away from their masters, when free again seek the same crib at which they used to feed.' Thus Posidonius, the Stoic, was wont to note in history that there were formerly many who, conscious of their own weakness, gave themselves, of their own accord, to be slaves to others (ὁπως παρ ἐκεινων, etc.), 'that they might receive from them the care and provision which they needed, and do them in return all the service they were able.' Others add an instance of this in the Mariandyni, who, for the same reason, made themselves slaves to the Heracleotæ."*

Hence it appears that slavery may be, and in fact, to a great extent, has been founded on the consent of the slaves; and a right to the service of persons founded on their own consent, is evidently agreeable to the law of Nature, being confirmed by that fundamental and immutable principle which requires men to be faithful to their engagements. They who maintain that government is founded on the consent of the people, maintain also that this consent is presumed when the contrary is not manifest, and that it is held to be tacit and implied in many cases in which it is not expressed; and is not to be set aside and overruled by individuals because of their particular complaints and grievances. In countries, therefore, where slavery exists, if the slaves are content with their lot and do not evidence the contrary by any overt act, it is not easy to see, on these principles, why their consent should not be presumed and regarded as the foundation of the masters' right, or why a right founded on tacit and general consent and exercised for

* Lib. ii., c. v., sect. 27.

the good of the whole, should fail or be voided because it happens to operate severely in particular cases. The fact that thousands of persons, and even whole tribes, have, of their own accord, subjected themselves to masters for the certainty of protection and maintenance, and surrendered their liberty for what they considered an equivalent in return, shows very plainly that all servitude is not involuntary and contrary to natural rights.

There are other ways in which slavery may originate without violation of justice. For, as men have a natural right to sell themselves, when they think it for their benefit to do so (*i. e.*, to make over to another their own labors for life, and the disposal of their persons, so far as necessary to secure their labors); and, as this practice has prevailed to a great extent, where it has not been prohibited by municipal law, so have fathers a natural right, in cases of necessity, to sell their own children. These are the words of Grotius, who has never been accused of being unfriendly to liberty. "Although," he says, "the paternal authority is so fixed and inherent in the father's person and character, that it can never be taken from him, and transferred to another; yet may a father *naturally*, and where the *civil law* does not obstruct it, *pawn* his child, and *sell* him too, if there be a necessity for it, and no other way of maintaining him." *

* And, in a note, he subjoins from Jornandes, in his Gothic history: "This is even what parents do here, who, consulting the preservation of their children, had much rather they should lose their freedom than

"And this right," he continues, "other nations seem to have borrowed from that Theban law, mentioned by Ælian in his second book, as the Thebans from the Phœnicians, and they, in turn, from the Hebrews; and Apollonius tells us, in his epistle to Domitian, that this very law obtained also among the Phrygians." Thus far Grotius; and the reason which he gives for his opinion, is worthy of note: "Nature itself is supposed to grant a right to every thing, without which that which she commands can not be accomplished."

But, although slavery was originally founded in contract, yet there can be no doubt that the number of slaves has been greatly enlarged, and their condition aggravated, by the fortunes of war. For, on the principles on which wars were anciently, and are still, in some countries, conducted, the lives of the conquered are at the mercy of the conqueror. The captive was believed, by the right of war, to have forfeited his life, and it was accounted an act of clemency to spare his life, on condition that it should be spent in the service of the captor. Hence *mancipia* (*manu capti, taken by hand*, or taken in battle) became a common appellation of slaves, and *emancipation* came to mean delivery from servitude. But the clemency, it should be observed, was extended

their lives; and, therefore, out of mere kindness, *sell* them for a maintenance, rather than keep them to starve and perish at home." To which he adds, "I find there has been the same custom among the people of Mexico." (See l. ii., c. 5, sect. 5.)

by the one party, and accepted by the other, on a given CONDITION; perpetual service being promised by the one, in return for his life being spared by the other. So that in this case, also, if we consider it carefully, we find that slavery was in reality founded on contract, and that the fortune of war merely furnished the occasion of the contract. If it be said, that the contract was morally void, because it was made on an erroneous principle, and under compulsion, I answer, that I am not concerned to defend it; for I by no means justify slavery on the ground of conquest. Only I would have it observed, how naturally the relation of the captor and the captured may be changed even during their lives (of the relations of their children I shall speak by-and-by), and the contract, which was at first the result of necessity, and extorted by fear, come, after a while, to be the offspring of choice, and cemented by good-will. For, when the contract was formed, both parties would find their mutual advantage in keeping it in good faith. For if the slave adhered to his natural right of liberty, and, in consequence of it, should seek opportunity to escape from service, and take the life of his master; in a word, if he persisted in regarding his master as his enemy, and acting towards him by the laws of war, why, then the master would assert his right by the same laws, to imprison the slave, to force him to hard labor, and even to take his life. It would, therefore, be for the interest of both parties to divest themselves of the *animus* of war, to lay aside their hostility, and to bind themselves, in good faith and by moral ties, to observe the compact by which master and slave are bound together in peaceable and friendly society; the same compact, in fact, which is the original and natural foundation of the relation. And, however some may deride, I can not but regard it as an illustration of the beneficence of God's providence (ever educing good out of evil), and of His wise adaptation of mankind to their condition in this world, that even that servitude, which, at first, springs from war, and is a violence to Nature, is suffered thus easily and naturally to pass into servitude in its peaceful and normal state; and men silently turned from enemies and destroyers into mutual helpers and friends.

CHAPTER VIII.

THE NATURAL JUSTICE OF SLAVERY INFERRED FROM THE CONSENT OF MANKIND: THE JUSTINIAN CODE.

In referring to the customs of former ages, I have no intention to hold them up as models for the imitation of the nineteenth century. We of this age possess, no doubt, many and great advantages over those that have preceded us; nor do I at all suppose that the antiquity of slavery is any proof of its excellence, or that the precedents of ancient Greece and Rome ought to bias a Christian people in its favor. Indeed, if the question were as to the eligibility of free or slave institutions, under circumstances equally favorable to both, and involving no *moral* obligation in behalf of either, I should feel no hesitation in avowing my preference for freedom, and my aversion to slavery. But I beg to remind the reader, again and again, that this is not the question which I have undertaken to discuss. It is not the *inexpediency*, but the pretended *injustice* of slavery, the deeply rooted, and wide-spread conviction among us, that slavery is upheld *merely* by local law in opposition to the law of Nature, or the dictates of universal justice;

it is this which has so exasperated one section of our country against the other, as to render it impossible for the two sections, while the baneful influence of this sentiment continues, to be united harmoniously under one government. It is to this conviction that I address myself. It is the moral right or justice of slavery, and not its advantages or disadvantages as compared with other forms of society, which I aim to establish. It is the fact (for such I believe it to be) that the *positive* and *local* laws which uphold slavery are not necessarily *repugnant to*, but may be *declarative of*, the law of Nature, which I have undertaken to prove. On a question of justice or injustice, on a question that involves the true meaning and intent of Natural law, the consent of nations ought to be decisive; and I hope, therefore, that the reader will permit me, before I come to the distinct consideration of that form of slavery which exists in our Southern States, to enlarge a little on the argument of our last chapter, which was designed to show that slavery may be founded in justice; and to remove, as I hope to do, an objection which has been of great force to strengthen the opposite conviction.

The Sacred History informs us, and I now appeal to it only for its testimony to facts, that slavery existed under the patriarchs for centuries before the conquest of Canaan, and that after the settlement of Canaan, it continued to exist among the Hebrews and the contiguous nations in times anterior to the records of profane history. From profane history, also, we learn that slavery existed among the Assyrians, Medes, and Persians, before the origin of the Grecian republics. The monuments of Greece and Rome leave no doubt that slavery existed in these republics from their infancy, and that it grew and flourished, so to speak, under the shadow of the tree of civil liberty. Nor was slavery extirpated from the empire when Rome became Christian, under Constantine. On the contrary, it was recognized by the Christian Church, and the mutual rights and duties involved in it were guarded by canons, which forbade slaves to be ordained, married, or baptized, without the consent of their owners, lest these acts should be made a pretext for defrauding the master of his right of property in the slave. In the changes of society that brought about the dissolution of the Roman empire, slavery was stripped of its more repulsive features, and gradually, to a great extent, decayed. But it was not wholly abolished. Since the Reformation, it has existed not only in the East, where it has always prevailed, but also in some parts of Europe; and although the nations of western Europe rejected it for themselves, they yet made no scruple to establish it in their American dependencies; and the abominable and infamous expedients to which they most unjustifiably resorted to introduce slave labor in places where it was demanded, and then not otherwise to be had, ought to suggest to us the folly and danger of attempting to subvert and expel it from places where it is equally needed, and has come to be naturally and peaceably established. These are facts which lie on the surface of history, and which, as I have rather understated them, it is the less necessary to prove by a citation of authorities.

And not only has slavery existed among these nations as a fact, but it has been intimately interwoven with the whole texture of their society. It was regulated by law among the Hebrews, Greeks, and Romans; Homer represents his heroes as exchanging slaves, as well as copper and iron, hides and cattle, for wine and provisions;* and all the poets, tragic, comic, and satirical, have not only borne testimony to the existence of slavery as a fact, but have derived from it occasions and incidents for pathetic description, for the keenest sallies of wit and shrewdness, and the most amusing illustrations of life and manners.

The wise men of Greece and Rome were thrown, for want of Divine Revelation, exclusively on the law of Nature. They investigated its principles with profound penetration, and deduced from them the duties of life by rigorous application of reason; and though their instructions failed of their due effect for want of being bound on the conscience by those awful sanctions which

* *ἔνθεν ἄῤ οἰνίζοντο καρηκομόωντες Ἀχαιοί,*
ἄλλοι μὲν χαλκῷ ἄλλοι δ' αἴθωνι σιδήρῳ,
ἄλλοι δὲ ῥινοῖς, ἄλλοι δ' αὐτῇσι βόεσσιν,
ἄλλοι δ' ἀνδραπόδεσσι·—*Iliad* vii., *vss.*, 472, etc.

only Divine Revelation can furnish, yet undoubtedly they did much to prepare the world for the candid consideration and cordial reception of Christian doctrine.

I am well aware that slavery in the ancient republics, particularly in Sparta and Rome, was accompanied with excessive violence and cruelty. This was the natural consequence of that *absolute* power, vested in the master, which Christianity, in later times, effectually *limited* by those *divine precepts* (transcending all the power of human suasion) which accustomed men to act more on the principles of justice and benevolence, and from a sense of responsibility to their MASTER in HEAVEN. But I am not aware that the ancient moralists, though they reproved the oppression and cruelty of masters in the treatment of their slaves, ever impugned the justice of the relation. On the contrary they assumed it, so far as my knowledge extends, to be just, and gave directions for its humane fulfillment. Under the modest title of "Offices," the wise men of antiquity set forth pithy treatises on the relative duties of life (or *offices*, as they were then called), which would better repay our study than some of the verbose elaborations which, under the sonorous titles of Systems of Moral Philosophy, and Elements of Moral Science, have enlarged only to impoverish the literature of our age. One of these treatises speaks the sentiments of all on the subject under consideration. "We ought to remember," says Cicero, "that we are bound to practise JUSTICE towards the lowest of mankind; the lowest, both in condition and fortune, are slaves; and they give us wholesome precepts who bid us treat our slaves as hired laborers, and make it our duty to exact of them labor, and to afford them in return the food, clothing, shelter, and protection which are due to them." *

Now I do not appeal to these facts as proofs that human society is in a healthier state with slavery than without it. It may be that slavery, as it has worn out in Great Britain, is destined also, in the progress of events, to expire universally, and to make room for something better in its place. It is not against measures designed to promote its natural decay (in places where it is in process of decay) that I contend, but against the manifold attempts that are now making to arrest and extirpate it, on the ground of its being an unjust institution, and at war with human rights. Will they who reject Revelation because it allows slavery, go farther and proclaim war upon the common sense of mankind? But for particular men, or even for a single age, to set up their own reason as the measure of all human reason, what is this better than insanity? Universal consent has ever been thought the most infallible criterion of truth; it is the strongest argument that can

* Meminerimus autem, etiam adversus infimos justitiam esse servandam. Est autem infima conditio et fortuna servorum, quibus non male præcipiunt qui ita jubent uti ut mercenariis; OPERAM EXIGENDAM, JUSTA PRÆBENDA.—*De Officiis*, Lib. i. c. xiii.

be brought, independently of Revelation, for the being of God, and the natural immortality of the human soul; the concurrence of all nations in these sentiments being evidently owing either to the traditions of an original Revelation, prior to all written revelations, or to the suggestions of Nature and the inborn rudiments of reason. There is no nation, ancient or modern, barbarous or civilized, heathen or Christian, which has not, by its laws, condemned the violation of compacts, the cruel oppression of the innocent, and the fraudulent withholding of his wages from the honest laborer. But where is the nation that has pronounced a state of servitude for life contrary to natural justice? What age, before our own, could point to moralists that proclaim it an offense against nature to hold slaves in the condition in which Providence has placed them? *operam exigere, justa præbere*, to exact of them labor, and to give them board, lodging, and raiment in compensation for their labor? And if slavery has, in fact, existed among most nations; if no nation has proclaimed it a violation of natural justice; and if the most eminent men of all time, legislators, sages, and moralists, have confessed a state of servitude for life, no matter what name they have given it, to be consistent with justice, then we have, to this extent, the consent of mankind in its favor; and from this consent we are entitled to infer, not indeed its expediency in every country and every state of society, but its agreement with, or non-repugnance to, the LAW OF NATURE.

But if this conclusion be correct, how comes the Justinian Code to define slavery as an institution of the law of nations *in opposition to natural justice?* This definition finds much favor with the lawyers who have lost in our day none of that laudable bias in favor of freedom, which Bodin, as I remember, in his synopsis of the arguments for and against slavery, ascribes to them in his time. From the lawyers the definition has passed into our horn-books and periodical journals, so that now every educated man is supposed to be aware of the fact that the Justinian Code—a great authority on a subject of this sort—declares slavery to be an abnormal state of society, upheld by force and in violation of justice.

Is it probable that a code, which it took centuries to mature, which is founded on the law of Nature, and is one of the ablest developments of its principles ever made by unassisted reason, has stultified itself by defending and protecting an institution which it proclaims in the outset to be contrary to that law? Is it not just possible that, in imputing to the code so flagrant an inconsistency, we may stultify ourselves?

Let us examine the authority. The passage occurs in the first book of the Institutes, near the beginning, and reads thus:

"Summa itaque divisio de jure personarum hæc est:

quod omnes homines aut liberi sunt, aut servi. Et libertas quidem (ex qua etiam liberi vocantur) est naturalis facultas ejus, quod cuique facere libet, nisi si quid vi aut jure prohibetur. *Servitus autem est constitutio juris gentium qua quis dominio alieno contra naturam subjicitur.*"

Which is translated as follows by Dr. Harris, in his edition of Justinian, with English notes, London, A. D. 1756:

"The first division of persons, with respect to their rights, is into freemen and slaves.

"Liberty, or freedom, from which we are denominated free, is that natural power which we have of acting as we please, if not hindered by force, or restrained by the law.

"Slavery is that, by which one man is made subject to another, according to the law of nations, though contrary to natural right."

It may be suggested by some, who read the original, that slavery is said to be *against Nature*, and not against the right or law of Nature. The word *Nature*, however, is commonly used for the right or law of Nature; and therefore I dismiss this criticism as unworthy of consideration, and accept Dr. Harris's translation.

It is to be observed, however, that the Code affixes to the phrase *law of Nature* a meaning different from that in which the phrase is commonly taken.

By the *law of Nature*, according to the best usage

among the ancients, and universally among the moderns, is meant, as we have said, that rule of fitness which the Deity has established for the government of men, considered as reasonable creatures, and intended for mutual society. But the code itself, in the chapter next before that which contains the definition of slavery, gives us its own definition of the law of Nature. Adopting the language of Ulpian it says expressly, under the title, "De Jure Naturali," etc.:

"The law of Nature is not a law to man only, but likewise to all other animals, whether they are produced on the earth, in the air, or in the waters. From hence proceeds the conjunction of male and female, which we, among our own species, style matrimony; from hence arises the procreation of children, and our care in bringing them up. We perceive also that the rest of the animal creation are regarded as having a knowledge of this law by which they are actuated." *

Now by the law of Nature, in this large sense of the phrase, man is as free as the beasts of the field; and to say that slavery is against Nature, or the law of Nature, in this sense, is merely to say that no precedent or

* In the text I have used Dr. Harris' version; the Latin is as follows: "Jus naturale est quod natura omnia animalia docuit; nam jus istud non humani generis proprium est, sed omnium animalium, quæ in cœlo, quæ in terra, quæ in mari nascuntur. Hinc descendit maris atque fœminæ conjunctio, quam nos matrimonium appellamus. Hinc liberorum procreatio, hinc educatio: videmus enim, cœtera quoque animalia istius juris peritia censeri."

analogy could then be drawn in favor of slavery from the brute creation. I say, could *then* be drawn in favor of slavery; for the ancients were undoubtedly ignorant of the astonishing facts which modern naturalists have brought to light in respect to a certain species of ants; and which, if then known, would have restrained them from saying that slavery was *contrary to Nature*, even in Ulpian's sense of the word. But they were ignorant of these curious facts, and they pronounced slavery contrary to Nature, on the supposition that no precedent or analogy in its favor could be drawn from the brute creation.*

* I annex from Harper's Family Library (No. VIII., p. 127), a passage, which contains a synopsis of these extraordinary discoveries—referring the reader to the note at the end of this chapter, for many interesting details. Among facts, all of which are wonderful, not the least remarkable and instructive is the mutual good-will and affection, which prevails between the negro ants and their masters, and that, too, mauger the fact that the relation had its origin in hostility and violence. Read the whole description at the end of this chapter.

"Connected with the subject of the warfare of ants is the history of a species of this insect, not existing in these islands, called, by Huber, the Amazon, or Legionary Ant, the *Formica rufescens* of Latreille. It is both warlike and powerful, and, unlike the rest of the tribe, its habits are far from being industrious. Enough has been said to show that the proceedings of some insects so nearly resemble human actions, as to excite our greatest wonder: but the habits of the legionary ant are still more surprising than the proceeding of the chiefs which we have just described; it is actually found to be a slave-dealer, attacking the nests of other species, stealing their young, rearing them, and thus, by shifting all the domestic duties of their republic on strangers, escaping from labor themselves. This curious fact, first discovered by Huber, has been confirmed by Latreille, and

But man is to be considered not only as an animal, but as a creature endowed with reason, as intended for society, as accountable for his actions, and as obliged to certain duties, which are devolved on him by the various relations in which he stands to his fellow-men, who are by nature his equals, to all his fellow-creatures on earth, and to God, the Maker of all. Hence, inasmuch as the Justinian Code applies the phrase, *law of Nature*, to those principles of action which are common to men and inferior creatures, we are naturally led to inquire, whether it had no distinctive name for that rule of action which is proper to man, considered as a reasonable and sociable creature? Certainly it had; and that name is the *Law of Nations.* Let the code speak for itself; the very next section to that last quoted is as follows:

"Civil law is distinguished from the law of nations, because every community uses partly its own particular laws, and partly the general laws, which are common to all mankind. That law which a people enacts for the

is admitted by all naturalists. The slave is distinguished from its master by being of a dark ash-color, so as to be entitled to the name of Negro—an epithet now appropriated to the *Formica fusca*, or ash-colored ants. Their masters are light in color. The negro is an industrious, peaceable, stingless insect; the legionary, a courageous, armed, and lazy one. The relation between them is not, however, that which exists between a task-master and his bondsman, but a strong attachment is mutually felt—another instance of the modification of instinct, education obliterating in the ash-colored ant all its natural antipathy to another species."

government of itself, is called the civil law of that people. But that law which natural reason appoints for all mankind, is called the law of Nations, because all nations make use of it."

Hence it appears that what the Justinian Code means by the law of Nations, is the same that we now mean by the law of Nature; viz., the rule which natural reason appoints for all mankind. In modern times, indeed, especially since the time of Grotius, the phrase *law of Nations* has been used to denote those rules and regulations by which the civilized nations govern their intercourse with one another. Among the ancients, however, the rules of international intercourse were too few in number, and too limited in application, to be wrought into a distinct science. Hence it very naturally happened that Tribonian, who digested the Justinian code, used the phrase *law of Nations* to distinguish the rule which natural reason prescribes to man from the *law of Nature* in the sense in which he found it used by Ulpian and other ancient lawyers. It is obvious to remark, however, that this use of the latter phrase, which had probably been borrowed from the poets and philosophers, is improper; in other words, that the wholesome lessons and examples which men may learn from their observation of inferior creatures, are not, in a proper sense, a law which they are obliged to obey. So sensible of this were the ancients, that many of them used the phrase *law of Nature* in its limited and proper sense; and what is remarkable is, that even the Code itself which is a collection from various sources, uses the phrase in one place at least, in the same sense. For (Tit. I Sec. 11), it refers the origin of dominion and property to the law of Nature; and adds, to leave no doubt of its meaning, "which, as we have already observed, *is also called* the law of Nations." No wonder, then, that the phrase *law of Nature* has come to be used universally by the moderns, as it was used to some extent by the ancients in its limited sense, to denote the rule of action proper to *human* nature; while the phrase *law of Nations* has been turned from the sense affixed to it in the Justinian Code, and appropriated to a branch of study which was unknown to the ancients.

"Ita verborum vetus interit ætas."

Mr. Maxwell, in his learned annotations on Bishop Cumberland (London, A. D. 1727), has placed this matter in a clear light. "The civilians," he remarks, "universally acknowledge, 'that the division into the *law of Nature* and that of *Nations*, according to Justinian's explication, is only the explaining two different senses of the same word;' the former *improper* and *metaphorical*, as Naturalists use the word *law*, to denote *those uniform effects which are observed in the motions of bodies.* The latter is *proper.* By the *law of Nature*, the Emperor understands only *uniform instincts observed in all animals;* by the *law of Nations* he denotes what our author, with most moderns and ancients, calls the *law of Nature.* Some later writers, by the *law of Nations,* understand that *branch of the law of Nature which relates to sovereign States, or princes,* or those conventions about certain privileges of ambassadors, about goods taken in open war, and certain limitations of the methods of hostility, to which, perhaps, antecedently to conventions express or tacit, there would have been no obligation."

The Justinian Code, therefore, is so far from affirming slavery to be repugnant to the law of Nature, in our sense of the expression, that it affirms the direct contrary. It declares slavery to be a constitution of the law of Nations, having previously defined this law to be *that which Natural Reason appoints for all mankind;* which is just what we now mean by the law of Nature. It denominates slavery a *constitution* or appointment, and thus distinguishes the relation of master and slave from those relations which exist naturally and without the intervention of any human act; and, to make this distinction more apparent, it adds that slavery is against Nature, or the law of Nature, inasmuch as it does not exist by nature, but is always brought about by some act or constitution of human reason. To illustrate: the relation of parent and child is natural; that is, it is not effected by any constitution or appointment of human reason or human law, but results from the very nature of the parties who, while they both live, are, and can not cease to be, parent and child. Not so, says the Code, with the relation of master and slave; for this relation does not exist by nature, nor result from the law of creation, but takes its beginning from some human act, and rests for support, not on the original law of creation, but on the constitution or appointment of that law which natural reason prescribes for the government of all mankind.

In this construction of the Code which makes slavery to be upheld by *positive* law considered as *declarative* of the law of Nature, I am confirmed by two passages of Grotius, with the quotation of which, and of a note by one of his commentators, I shall conclude this chapter. In the second book of his great work (De Jure Belli, etc.) chap. 22, § 11, Grotius observes that, "To take up arms on account of liberty is not justifiable either in particular persons or in a whole community, as if to be in such a state—a state, that is, of *autonomy*, or independence—were *naturally* and *at all times* every one's prerogative. For when men are said to be *by nature* in a state of freedom, *by nature* must be understood to mean the right of Nature *as it is antecedent to all human acts to the contrary;* and the freedom there meant is a freedom in a *privative* not in a *contradictory* sense; that is to say, though a man be not *by nature* a slave, or subject to any, yet he can not thence derive a right of being always exempted from slavery and subjection; for in this sense nobody living is free. And this is what Albutius intends when he says that no man is born either a freeman or a slave, but these names fortune gives them afterwards. Thus Aristotle *Νόμῳ το μεν δόυλον ειναι το δε ελέυθερον*, 'To the law it is owing that one man is in a free, another in a servile condition.'" *

And again, in the third book of the same work, at the beginning of the seventh chapter, the same author says:

"No man is a slave by nature, that is, without any human deed, and considered in the primitive state of nature; as we have elsewhere said: in which sense we may take the lawyers when they say that slavery is against Nature. That slavery, however, should take its origin from some human act, is not, as we have elsewhere shown, repugnant to natural justice." †

On which passage, in reference to the words *against Nature*, Gronovius observes: That slavery is opposed to

* "Sed nec libertas, sive singulorum sive civitatum, id est *αὐτονομία*, quasi naturaliter, et semper quibusvis competat, jus bello præstare potest. Nam libertas cum natura competere hominibus aut populis dicitur, id intelligendum est de jure naturæ præcedente factum omne humanum, et de libertate *κατα στέρησιν*, non de ea quæ est *κατ' ἐναντιότητα*, hoc est, ut natura quis servus non sit, non ut jus habeat ne unquam serviat; nam hoc sensu nemo liber est: quo pertinet illud Albutii; 'neminem natura liberum esse, neminem servum; hæc postea nomina singulis imposuisse fortunam.' Et Aristotelis illud: *Νόμῳ το μεν δόυλον ειναι, το δε ελέυθερον*; e lege venisse ut alius esset liber, alius servus."

† Servi natura quidem, id est, citra factum humanum aut primævo naturæ statu, hominum nulli sunt, ut et alibi diximus; quo sensu recte accipi potest quod a juris-consultis dictum est, contra naturam esse hanc servitutem: ut tamen facto hominis, id est, pactione aut delicto, servitus originem acciperet, justitiæ naturali non repugnat, ut alibi quoque ostendimus.

liberty, and that liberty is an endowment of Nature; it being understood, however, that Nature has not bestowed this endowment on men in such sense as to prevent some from being for just causes deprived of it; for the endowment is not inalienable, but may be lost by fault or fortune.*

N. B.—The author quoted in the note, pp. 113, 114, remarks that all we know concerning the negro ant is derived from Mr. P. Huber, and he adds the following short summary of Huber's account;

"While walking near Geneva, between four and five in the evening of the 17th of June, 1804, this distinguished naturalist observed an army of the rúfescent or legionary ants traversing the road. The column occupied a space of ten inches in length, by four in breadth; they rapidly quitted the road, passed a thick hedge, entered a pasture-ground, wound through the grass without breaking the line of march, and approached a nest inhabited by the negro or ash-colored ant. Some of its inhabitants were guarding the entrance, but on the discovery of an approaching army, they darted forth on the advancing party. The alarm was communicated to the interior, whence their companions rushed in numbers to join in the defense of their underground residence. The bulk of the army of the legionaries being about two paces off, now quickened their march, and in an instant the whole battalion fell upon and overthrew the negroes, who, after a short and obstinate conflict, retired and took refuge in the lowest parts of their nest. The legionaries now mounted the hillock; some took possession of the principal avenues, while others effected a new breach with their teeth, so as to admit the remainder of the army. Having thus taken the city by assault, they remained in it only a few minutes: returning by the apertures through which they had entered, each carried in its mouth either a larva or a pupa, and scampered away without order or regularity. M. Huber followed them for some

* Servitutem esse contrariam illi bono, quod contigit homini beneficio naturæ et per naturam, id est libertati; quamvis id ita ei natura dederit, ut ob justas causas eripi non vetet; ut sit bonum separabile, quod peccato aut fortuna possit amitti.

time, but lost sight of them in a cornfield. Wishing to observe the assaulted city again, he retraced his steps, and saw a small number of ash-colored laborers perched on the stalks of plants, holding in their mouths the few larvæ which they had succeeded in rescuing from pillage.

The next morning, Huber, taking the same road, with the hope of once more seeing a similar scene, discovered a large ant-hill tenanted by legionaries. At five in the evening, provided the weather be fine, and the temperature 67° Fahrenheit in the shade, these sally out. During the other part of the day they appear to do little; but at this hour they become restless, assemble on the outside of the city, move round it in circles: a signal is then given, which they pass from one to the other, striking, as they proceed, with their antennæ and forehead, the breasts of their companions; these, in their turn, approach those advancing, and communicate the same signal—it is that of departure—as the result satisfactorily proves. Those which receive the intimation are instantly seen to put themselves on the march; the column becomes organized; and not a single amazon remains near the garrison. There is no commander-in-chief; every ant is in turn first, each seeking to be foremost. A small number may, however, be observed constantly returning to the rear: this is probably the means by which the whole army is governed.

With such dispositions, maneuvers, and discipline, Huber saw an army of legionaries set out for a negro city. With their usual impetuosity of attack, one party soon entered, and returned laden with the young of the assailed ant-hill; a second detachment, not meeting with equal success, separated from their companions, and fell on another negro colony, where they met with ample booty; after which the whole number of legionaries marched to their nest in two divisions. As they approached, Huber saw, to his astonishment, a great number of the very same species which had been pillaged, all around the nest of the legionaries. Was this a diversion made by carrying the war into the enemy's territory? No: the return of the legionaries excited no alarm; on the contrary, the negro ants were seen to approach these warriors, caress them with their antennæ, offer them nourishment, as is the custom among their own species, while the legionaries consigned their prisoners to them to be carried to the interior of the nest.

In this way the same negro colony was observed to be attacked three several times, and each time with complete success; the last attack, however, was made under different circumstances from the first two: the negroes, as if conscious of their exposed situation, had lost no time in throwing up trenches, barricading the several entrances, and reënforcing the guard of the interior; "they had, moreover, brought together all the little pieces of wood and earth within their reach; with these they had blocked up the passage to their habitation, in which they had posted themselves in full force."

"The legionaries at first hesitating to approach, rambled about or returned to the rear; they then on a given signal rushed forward *en masse*, with great impetuosity, removing with their teeth and feet the many obstacles which impeded their progress; having succeeded, they entered the ant-hill by hundreds, notwithstanding the resistance of its inhabitants, and carried off their prize to the garrison."

In these attacks the legionaries never take the old negroes prisoners, knowing, perhaps, that at an adult age the love of home, with all its associations, would be sad obstacles to transplantation; nor is their contest attended with loss of blood; they seek the young, and these being obtained, they speedily decamp with their booty. Nor do they ever begin their predatory warfare before the end of May, or beginning of June; if they commenced at an earlier period to purloin the young negroes, they might secure a large supply of captives, but then it would principally consist of males and females, and these, it seems, Nature does not permit them to seize: for she has ordained that, in the ant-hills destined to pillage, the males and females shall be produced earlier than the males and females of the legionaries; and it is only after their own males and females have undergone the last change, that the instinct which prompts them to steal the young of others begins to operate. Hence, Huber has distinctly ascertained, and Latreille has confirmed the discovery, that the legionary ant-hill contains male, female, and neuter amazons, together with negro-neuters, but never negro males or females. The *amazon* female, after having cast off her wings, lays the foundation of her own nest, and performs all the duties of a laborer. There is no doubt that these creatures have the ability to work, and do so; but as soon as they obtain slaves to do that for them which they ought to do themselves, they relinquish every domestic duty, and during the day "tranquilly wait, at the bottom of their subterranean abode, the hour of departure, reserving their strength, courage, and the address which they so well know how to display, for the purposes of war."

On the negroes reared among them they depend not only for house and home, but even for food; and these faithful and affectionate servants begrudge neither labor nor pains, in providing for their masters. Huber enclosed thirty amazons with several pupæ and larvæ of their own species, and twenty negro pupæ, in a glass box, the bottom of which was covered with a thick layer of earth; honey was given to them, so that, although cut off from their auxiliaries, the amazons had both shelter and food: at first they appeared to pay some little attention to the young; this soon ceased, and they neither traced out a dwelling, nor took any food; in two days one-half died of hunger, and the other remained weak and languid: commiserating their condition, he gave them *one* of their black companions: this little creature, unassisted, formed a chamber in the earth, gathered together the larvæ, put everything into complete order, and preserved the lives of those which were about to perish.

In order to obtain a more intimate knowledge of the facts, the same observer of nature opened and deranged an ant-hill in which the negroes and amazons dwelt together; in doing so, the aspect of their city was so altered as not to be recognized by the amazons, and they were seen wandering at random over its surface. The negroes, however, appeared to be well acquainted with the new localities of the ant-hill, and relieved them from their embarrassment by taking them up gently in their mandibles, and conducting them to the galleries already pierced. "An amazon was frequently seen to approach a negro, and play upon its head with its antennæ, when the latter immediately seized the former in its pincers, and deposited it at one of the entrances; the amazon ant then unrolled itself, caressed once more its kind friend, and passed into the interior of the nest; now and then the negro lost its way too, and wandered about carrying the amazon.

"I observed one," continues Huber, "after ineffectual windings, take the precaution of laying its burden on the ground: the amazon remained on the same spot until the negro returned to its assistance, which, having well ascertained and examined one of the entrances, resumed its load, and bore it into the interior."

If the entrance to any gallery happened to be obstructed, the negro, depositing its burden, went to remove the obstruction, and again taking up the amazon, introduced it into the nest. It often happens that the ant-hill is not sufficiently commodious; in this case the negroes alone decide upon the expediency of a removal, and choose a spot for the new dwelling; they set about building, and as soon as the works are sufficiently advanced, appear eager to conduct the legionaries to the new city: for this purpose, each negro takes up an amazon, which it carries to the chosen spot, so that a long line of these faithful creatures may be seen extending all the way from the old to the new town; their charges are then deposited at the various entrances, when other negroes come out, welcome their arrival, and usher them into the interior of their new abode.

The negro is not the only species of ant subjugated by the legionaries. The mining ants are attacked for a similar purpose; but as these are a much more resolute race than the pacific ash-colored tribe, the legionaries are obliged to vary their tactics.

"In one of these forays, the amazons," says Huber, "proceeded like a torrent along a deep dike, and marched in a more compact body than ordinary, and in a short time reached the nest they proposed to attack. As soon as the legionaries began entering the subterranean city, the miners rushed out in crowds, and while some fell upon the invaders with great spirit, others passed through the scene of contest, solely occupied in bearing off to a place of safety their larvæ and pupæ."

The amazon army was often despoiled of its booty, but their superior address and agility at length gave them the advantage, and in a quarter of an hour they were seen returning homewards loaded with prey—not, however, straggling, and in a file, as after an assault upon the negroes, but in a compact mass; a precaution so much the more necessary, as the courageous miners disputed every inch of ground, following and attacking them until they arrived within ten paces of the amazonian citadel.

Besides the amazons, there is another slave-making species, called the *formica sanguinea;* a species which has not as yet been discovered in this island. They are larger than the legionaries; unlike them, however, they share the labor with their slaves. Their mode of attack is very different from that of the legionaries; the latter carry every thing by sheer impetuosity; the former never pour in immense masses, but attack in small divisions; they sometimes go one hundred and fifty paces, to attack a negro habitation, and the various divisions succeed each other by means of couriers, which are evidently sent off to fetch assistance from the garrison.

"On the 15th of July, at 10 A. M.," says Huber, "a small division of sanguine ants was despatched from the garrison, and arrived in quick march near a nest of negro ants, situated twenty paces distant, around which they took their station. The inhabitants, perceiving the strangers, rushed forth, and made several prisoners; the sanguine ants advanced no further: they appeared to be waiting for reënforcements; from time to time, little companies arrived from the garrison to strengthen the brigade: thus reunited they advanced a little nearer and seemed more willing to run the risk of a general engagement; but in proportion as they approached the negro dwelling, the more solicitous did they seem to despatch couriers to the garrison, who, arriving in great haste, produced considerable alarm, when another division was immediately despatched to join the army. The negroes took up a position of about two feet square, in front of their nest, where nearly their whole force was assembled, awaiting the enemy." In the interim, the pupæ were removed to the side of the nest facing the field of battle, so that they might be conveyed away at a moment's warning, affording a trait of what Huber calls prudence, and certainly a marvelously singular one it is. When fighting with the amazons, the impetuosity of the attack leaves the negro ant no time for thought, but in their contests with the sanguine ants, they vary their tactics so as to meet the new circumstances. The latter insects, being sufficiently reënforced, make the attack, and band after band pillage, and carry away their booty, not in a few minutes, as is done by the amazons, but during the whole day; and if the pillaged city should suit them better than their own, they remove to it on the following morning; at least so it appears in an instance observed by Huber. It is rare, according to that author, that they do not change at least once during the year. They certainly inspire the negroes with great terror, for these, once attacked by them, generally forsake their nest for ever.

"To their own slaves they are much attached; the sanguine ants are often besieged by the fallow ants: on these occasions they carry their servants to the lowest chambers, and these, as if aware of the intention of their removal, immediately begin barricading the different entrances, with every species of material lying within their reach.

The sanguine ants evince extraordinary foresight in these engagements; for, while one party is fighting, another is engaged in bearing away the negroes, who immediately begin by constructing a new dwelling at a considerable distance from the scene of combat."

Such is the extraordinary recital contained in that delightful work of Huber's, every fact of which has been confirmed by the subsequent observations of the accurate and learned Latreille. It would seem that the negro and miner ants are both occasionally enslaved, and dwell together in the sanguine ant-hills. And Huber has brought up legionaries and sanguine ants, which are both slave-makers, with negroes, in one common dwelling.

CHAPTER IX.

SLAVERY REGARDED AS A PROVIDENTIAL INSTITUTION.

HAVING shown that slavery may be introduced into human society without violence to justice, and that even when it originates in war, it passes by a tendency of human nature, amounting almost to a law, into a peaceful and orderly form of society, I come now to show that, having been once introduced, it extends itself consistently with justice, and by the ordinary laws of Nature and Providence, unless its extension is violently arrested by some exterior agency. I do not mean that slavery is destined to be perpetual in every country in which it is planted: it partakes, we know, of the mutability of all things human; it rises and grows to maturity, remains stationary for a time, and then decays and dies out in conformity with certain laws which history, by its large induction of facts, enables us to perceive and unfold. But I mean that slavery once introduced becomes a just and settled institution of society; liable, indeed, to the changes effected by violent revolutions, or by other causes slower in their operation, and of a more insidious nature; but still a fixed social institution, entitled, while it lasts, in a degree proportioned to its importance, to the same religious regard which is paid by all good men, with common consent, to the orderly institutions of society, not only in their own country, but in every country on earth.

In the first place, as a presumptive, though not, I confess, a conclusive argument in favor of a derivative servitude from parent to child, I desire it may be considered that children, as a general rule, follow the condition of their parents; as, for example, that the children of the Arabs are Arabians, and that the natives of New England are not savages, like the aboriginal Indians, but are an enlightened, civilized, and Christian people, after the fashion of their Puritan forefathers. No man can deny the fact, and all my readers, I trust, will agree with me in ascribing it to the wise order of that Divine Providence which governs the world. The posterity of Abraham inherited, by this Divine Providence, the privileges which their father's faith had earned for them, as well as for himself; the descendants of Ham have been born to the curse pronounced on their progenitor; and, universally, from Pekin to Boston, from Cape Horn to Labrador, and from the time of Adam to the present day, children have, as a general rule, followed the condition of their parents; reaping in some instances the happy fruits of their piety and virtue, and exemplifying in other instances, the misery entailed on them by the follies and iniquities of the generation that preceded them.

What would be thought of the man who should wail over the hard lot of the children of the Esquimaux, because they were not born in France and Germany, or shed tears of compassion over the Musquito Indians, because they could enjoy only the "protection" of England, and were debarred, by the misfortune of their birth, from all participation in the liberties bestowed on her, by "our Great Deliverer," as Lord John Russell calls the Dutch William? Why, then, should it be esteemed either a wrong or a grievance that the children of slaves are not born to civil freedom? I say, *civil* freedom, since the only freedom to which they are not born is a certain civil state or condition; for, as to *natural* freedom, all men are born alike; and we do not need the Declaration of Independence to tell us that new-born infants, whether they first see the light in London or in Timbuctoo, in a king's palace or a slave's cabin, are all equal by nature. The parents of slaves are not more in a state of nature than their masters; they are equally with them members of civil society, only standing in a different relation to society.

The difference, then, between the children of slaves and the children of their masters being not a difference of Nature (for in this respect both are equal), but a difference of condition in human society, what reason, I ask again, has any man to wail and mourn over the sad condition of the children of slaves because they are not born to civil freedom? It is no more an impeachment of God's justice (for really it is God's Providence, and not man's agency, against which this objection is leveled) —it is, I say, no more an impeachment of God's justice and goodness that *men* should be born unequal in *fortune*, than that divers orders of *creatures* should be made unequal in nature. Whatever any creature has that is *positive*, either by its nature or condition, is to be ascribed to the bounty of the All Glorious Giver; whatever any creature is not or has not, is a mere *negation*, and to be ascribed, not to any defect of God's goodness, but to the original *nonentity* out of which the creature was produced. And, if it be an illustration of the wisdom and benevolence of the Deity, that He has made an infinite variety of creatures of divers kinds, how is it an impeachment of His Providence that He permits the greatest possible diversity of fortune or condition among creatures of the same kind? Why the condition of horses should be diversified; why some of the noble animals should be trained to the turf, or pampered for a nabob's chariot, while others, their equals in all the essentials of the equine nature, should be degraded to the dray, and doomed to be starved and beaten by some brute of an owner, it might puzzle a philosopher to explain. But man, who is placed in this world on probation for the future, whose character is capable of an infinite variety of development, and needs a corresponding variety of circumstances in order to its development—why should it be thought strange that his natural equality should be checkered with an infinite diversity of fortune? Must we raise the heathen from the dead to teach the nineteenth century Christians that the choice of our lot is not in ourselves but in God, and that it becomes us to act well our own part in life because it is that which the Master of the drama has assigned to us?*

Do our philanthropists really think that every human being has not scope enough for virtue in the rank and station in which God has placed him, that they are thus forever moving Acheron to make men as equal in fortune and condition as they are in nature? Is it not enough for woman to cultivate the grace and gentleness proper to her sex? Is the English collier incapable of all virtue, because he is not born a peer of the realm? Are all the civilities and charities and amenities of life of necessity bound up with that structure of society which exalts the individual—man, woman, or child—above the State, and can they only grace the car of that heaven-defying liberty which this sort of republicans have chosen for their tutelary goddess? Are there no virtues; nay, rather, are there not many of the noblest virtues and charities, and among them that divine and

* *Μέμνησο, ὅτι ὑποκριτὴς εἶ δράματος, οἵου ἂν θέλῃ ὁ διδάσκαλος· ἂν βραχὺ, βραχέος· ἂν μακρὸν, μακροῦ, ἂν πτωχὸν ὑποκρίνασθαί σε θέλῃ, ἵνα καὶ τοῦτον εὐφυῶς ὑποκρίνῃ· ἂν χωλὸν, ἂν ἄρχοντα, ἂν ἰδιώτην, σὸν γὰρ τοῦτ' ἔστι, τὸ δοθὲν ὑπυκρίνασθαι πυόσωπον καλῶς· ἐκλέξασθαι δ' αὐτὸ, ἄλλου.*—Epict. *Εγχειρ.* c. 17.

chastened liberty which God most approves, which either grow exclusively out of the relation of master and servant, or are indebted to it for their fuller expansion? It is a narrow view which limits all the virtues to one form of society; some flourish best on one soil, some on another; and all of them, in all their successive stages and manifold forms of development, are necessary to a complete humanity. Faith in God's providence should teach us, that He has so ordered the birth of every human being as to place him in that condition and those circumstances which he sees to be best for him, both as to this world and the world to come; and that he who is lowest (to the eye of man) in the scale of fortune, has infinitely more reason to be thankful for his humanity than to be discontented with his lot in life. And so men would think, if they were permitted to receive the gospel of Christ without the fumes of Exeter Hall and the everlasting din and clatter of fanatical busy-bodies.

But, it may be said, all other children have, indeed, no cause to complain that they follow the condition of their parents, because, whatever be its hardships, they are at least allowed their natural rights; but the children of slaves differ herein from all others, that they are at once, and as soon as born, deprived of their natural rights. This is a mistake; they are not deprived of their natural rights, but are protected in them by the masters, in whose service they are born, just as children, born free, are protected in *their* natural rights by their parents. But let us look at the matter, for a moment, on the popular supposition, and see what it will come to. "O that the children of slaves," you exclaim, "had but their natural rights, I would ask no more!" Nay, my dear reader, you shall have more. I will be as liberal to you as was the good fairy to the honest couple in the nursery tale. I will give you three wishes, and, my word for it, your third wish, like that of the said honest couple, will be prompted by the vanity of the two others. You wish that the children of the slaves might have their natural rights. Done! And now let me ask what have you gained for them? What provision does Nature make for them? She gives them the light of the sun by day, and the light of the moon and stars by night, and the air of heaven to breathe. This is their freedom by nature, and to these rights they are born. But how long will they live to enjoy this natural freedom without food, and shelter, and clothing? The young of brutes may soon take care of themselves, but the offspring of human parents are utterly helpless; they must be indebted for years to the care of others for maintenance, before they can provide for themselves.

The result, then, of your first wish is, that you leave the children to perish! Your second wish is, I suppose, that their parents also may have the rights of nature, so as to be at liberty to take care of their offspring. Agreed! Take away, then, from the parents the advantages they have received from their masters and from that intercourse with human society which they have enjoyed through their masters, and restore them to their pure and inalienable natural rights. Can more miserable creatures be imagined? Naked, and without the use of language, they pluck herbs and roots, and gather wild fruits; quench their thirst at the next spring, river, or ditch; and shelter themselves from the injuries of the weather by creeping into some cave, or covering themselves after any sort with moss, or grass; pass away their tedious life in idleness; start at every noise, and are afraid at the sight of any other animal; and perish at last, either by hunger or cold, or some wild beast. Oh, the blessed rights of Nature! And now, reader, tell me honestly whether your third wish will not be to revoke the two former wishes, and to restore these poor infants to the masters to whose care the good providence of God has committed them? For, believe me, God has never dealt so harshly with the descendants of Adam since the fall, as to leave them to their natural rights alone. Look the world through, and you will find that Nature, to use the words of the elder Pliny, has acted the part, rather of a cruel step-dame, than of a kind mother to the young of human parents; and that the *providence* of Almighty God has been far more bountiful than *Nature* to the children of our American slaves, by giving them Christian masters, who, from motives both of duty and interest, provide for their helpless infancy, and thus justly bind them to their service in their maturer years.

But before we proceed with the argument, the mention of the elder Pliny leads me to pause for a moment and invite the reader to refresh himself with one of the most remarkable passages of heathen antiquity. This great naturalist, having surveyed all inanimate creation, enters, in the seventh book of his Natural History, on the description of living creatures. And here, in the first place, his attention is arrested by the fact just referred to—the singular helplessness and wretchedness of human infancy. To us Christians, who have been instructed in the fall and redemption of man, the fact is not inexplicable; but to this inquisitive and intelligent heathen it was a mystery and a marvel; and the perplexity which it gave him probably excited him to study and exhibit the fact with a force and fullness which no Christian divine, to my knowledge, has ever equaled. I give the passage in the telling old English of a Church of England divine of the seventeenth century; and although it be not exactly the material for a fourth of July oration, it will yet prove, I trust, at least equally suggestive of salutary thoughts:

"Thus, as you see, we have in the former books sufficiently treated of the universal world, of the lands, regions, nations, seas, islands, and renowned cities therein contained. It remaineth now to discourse of the living creatures comprised within the same, and their natures:

a point, doubtless, that would require as deep a speculation as any part else thereof whatsoever, if so be the spirit and mind of man were able to comprehend and compass all things in the world. And to make a good entrance into this treatise and history, methinks of right we ought to begin at *Man*, for whose sake it would seem that Nature produced all other creatures besides: though this great favor of hers, so bountiful and beneficial in that respect, hath cost full dear. Insomuch as it is hard to judge, whether in so doing, she hath done the part of a kind mother, or an hard and cruel step-dame. For, first and foremost of all other living creatures, man she hath brought forth all naked, and clothed him with the good and riches of others. To all the rest given she hath sufficient to clad (clothe) them every one, according to their kind: as, namely, shells, cods, hard hides, pricks, shags, bristles, hair, down, feathers, quills, scales, and fleeces of wool. The very trunks and stems of trees and plants she hath defended with bark and rind, yea, and the same sometimes double, against the injuries both of heat and cold. Man alone, poor wretch, she hath laid all naked upon the bare earth, even on his birth-day, to cry and wrawl presently from the very first hour that he is born into this world: in such sort as, among so many living creatures, there is none subject to shed tears and weep like him. And, verily, to no babe or infant is given once to laugh before he be forty days old, and that is counted very early, and with the soonest.

Moreover, so soon as he is entered in this manner to enjoy the light of the sun, see how he is immediately tied and bound fast, and hath no member at liberty; a thing that is not practised upon the young whelps of any beast among us, be he never so wild. The child of man, so untowardly born, and who another day is to rule and command all other, lo how he lieth bound hand and foot, weeping and crying, and beginning his life with misery, as if he were to make amends and justification by his punishment unto Nature, for his only fault and trespass, that he is born and brought into the world. O folly of all follies, ever to think (considering this simple beginning of ours) that we were sent into this world to live in pride, and carry our head aloft! The first hope that we conceive of our strength, the first gift that time affordeth us, maketh us no better than four-footed beasts; how long is it ere we can go alone! How long before we can prattle and speak, feed ourselves and chew our meat strongly! What a while continueth the mold and crown of our heads to beat and pant, before our brain is well settled; the undoubted mark and token that bewrayeth our exceeding great weakness above all other creatures. What should I say of the infirmities and sickness that soon seize upon our feeble bodies? What need I speak of so many medicines and remedies devised against these maladies? besides the new diseases that come every day, to check and frustrate all our provision of physic whatsoever. As for all other living creatures there is not one, but by a secret instinct of nature knoweth his own good, and whereto he is made able: some make use of their swift feet, others of their flight wings; some are strong of limbs, others are apt to swim, and practice the same: man only knoweth nothing, except he be taught; he can neither speak, nor go, nor eat, otherwise than he is trained to it; and to be short, apt and good at nothing he is naturally, but to pule and cry.

"And hereupon it is, that some have been of this opinion, That better it had been, and simply best for man, never to have been born, or else speedily to die. None but we do sorrow and wail, none but we are given to excess and superfluity, infinitely in everything, and show the same in every member that we have. Who but we, again, are ambitious and vainglorious? Who but we are covetous and greedy of gathering good? We, and none but we, desire to live long, and never to die, are superstitious, careful of our sepulture and burial, yea, and what shall betide us when we are gone. Man's life is most frail of all others, and in least security he liveth: no creature lusteth more after everything than he; none feareth like unto him, and is more troubled and amazed in his fright; and if he be set once upon anger, none more raging and wood (mad) than he. To conclude, all other living creatures live orderly and well, after their own kind; we see them flock and gather together, and ready to make head and stand against all others of a contrary kind; the lions, as fell and savage as they be, fight not with one another; serpents sting not serpents, nor bite one another with their venomous teeth; nay, the very monsters and huge fishes of the sea, war not amongst themselves in their own kind; but, believe me, man, at man's hand, receiveth most harm and mischief." *

* Jaçkson's Works, fol. ed., vol. iii., b. 10, c. 8. For the original, see Appendix.

CHAPTER X.

AMERICAN SLAVERY CONSIDERED AS A SOCIAL INSTITUTION.

BUT to return to our argument. We have seen that the contract which tacitly subsists between the master and his slaves devolves on the one party the duty of care and protection, and on the other party the duty of service. Now the children of slaves are naturally part of their parents—bone of their bone, and flesh of their flesh. Naturally, therefore, as well as justly, and by a moral necessity, they become parties to the contract that subsists between their parents and the master. That infants, as soon as born, are incapable of becoming parties to a contract, will be affirmed by no person who is even moderately conversant with moral science. The consent and custom of all nations; the theories of the profoundest authors on the constitution of human society; the divinely prescribed usage of the Jewish Church; the entire consent of the Christian Church; and, with few exceptions, of all professing Christians, from the time of the Apostles to the present, concurring with the Jewish Church in not only recognizing infants as capable of a covenant relation, but in formally sealing and ratifying that relation, put it out of all doubt that infants may be justly held to be parties to a contract for their own benefit. As respects the children of slaves, it is so obviously beneficent, so clearly just, so imperatively obligatory to admit them to the same contract with their parents, that the master who should refuse them this boon, who should turn them off his hands, where the providence of God has placed them, and throw them back on the mere rights of Nature, instead of according to them the more sacred and important rights that justly accrue to them by their birth of parents in his service; who, in a word, should leave them to perish, instead of providing for their wants, would be branded, and justly, as a monster of impiety, injustice, and cruelty. He can not escape from his responsibility without bringing on himself the displeasure of God and the scorn and execration of men; he is morally and religiously bound by ties of the most sacred nature, to provide for the wants of these infants, to feed and to lodge them, and to train them for the duties of their humble station.

You say that it is his interest to rear them, and that he does it from sordid motives, and in order to enrich himself by their future labor. I answer that his motives concern nobody but himself and his Maker; and as to his profiting by their labors, how unreasonable to carp at a man for not declining a duty because the Providence of God has made it his interest to discharge it! Hard, indeed, would be our lot if we were compelled to work, either for this world or the next, without the hope of reward!

Now if it be granted, and I see not how it can be fairly denied, that the master is bound to extend support and maintenance to the children of his slaves during their infancy, then it inevitably follows that these children are indebted to him for this support and maintenance; and since he gives them support on condition of their future service, and they can not otherwise repay the debt, it follows that they owe him service as soon as they are capable of rendering it; nor is it just or equitable that they should quit his service unless they pay him an equivalent for his care and nurture. Thus the bond of servitude is formed by Providence; it is the offspring not of a physical but of a moral necessity, that is to say, not of arbitrary power but of benevolence and justice; it is formed under circumstances under which it can not but be formed without impiety to God and injustice to man; it is formed on the one part in infancy and helplessness, and is, therefore, next in sacredness to the ties of blood; and for the State to step in and annul the relation and cancel the real though implied contract, without the mutual consent of the parties, would be, as it seems to me, a stretch of arbitrary power that could only be justified by the same law of expediency and physical force on which slavery itself is thought, by many, to rest for its support.

That I may not be thought to be broaching any private fancies of my own, I beg to fortify my positions with the names of men, whose authority alone, I am not ashamed to confess, would silence my objections, even if their arguments failed to carry conviction to my reason.

The illustrious Grotius, after having mooted the question, not essential to our present argument, whether children are required by the law of Nature to follow the condition of the father or the mother on the supposition that the one was free and the other a slave; the Civil law, as is well known, making the child take its condition from the mother, the old English law from the father, the Saxons and some other nations from the slave parent, whether father or mother, and the West Gothic law, in case the parents belonged to different masters, requiring the value of the issue to be divided in two equal parts between the respective masters; Grotius, I say, having adverted to the difficulties involved in this question, with which we have no occasion to encumber our present inquiry, proceeds as follows:

"Let us suppose, then, for the ease of the inquiry, that both parents are slaves, and let us see whether so their children would be naturally slaves too. If there were, indeed, no other way of maintaining their children, parents might, with *themselves*, bring their *future* progeny into slavery; because, upon the very same account, parents may even *sell* their *free-born* children. But since this *right* does naturally arise from mere *necessity*, it is in no other circumstances allowed that *parents* should enslave their children; nor have *masters* any other *right* over the children of their slaves, than as they are to find them victuals and other necessaries of life; and, therefore, when the *children of slaves* have been for a long time maintained before they are capable of being serviceable to their *master*, and their work *then* can only answer the expense of their present maintenance, such children can never quit their service, unless they pay what is reasonable for all their former entertainment." *

Puffendorf, a name of equal weight with Grotius, and who wrote after him is still more explicit and cogent:

"It is easy to show that the master doth no *injury* to his slave's offspring, by dooming it to the same subjection. For, since the mother hath nothing of her own, it is impossible she should maintain the child but with the master's goods. And, inasmuch as the master is obliged to furnish such an infant with food, and other necessaries, long before he is capable of making any requital for his labor; and since, when he first begins to work, his pains are scarce equivalent to his daily maintenance, he can not escape servitude, unless by the master's particular dispensation. And this reason will hold, not only while he is supposed to continue, as it were, in the master's debt, but ever after; because the

* Right of War and Peace, Book II., c. v., sect. xxix., paragraphs 1 and 2.

condition, on which the master first undertook to keep him, was, that he should perform perpetual service, and to this condition he is presumed to have yielded his tacit consent; especially, if it be considered that his very birth is owing to his master's favor, who, by the right of war, might have put his parents to death. And as for that natural freedom, with which all men are in common invested, it then only takes place, when no act or agreement of ourselves or others, hath rendered us obnoxious to a state of inferiority." *

From all which it appears that, wherever slavery exists as a settled condition or institution of society, the bond which unites master and servant is of a *moral* nature; founded in *right*, not in *might;* and obligatory on the conscience, as really so as the bond that unites men in the higher and more sacred relations of life. Let the origin of the relation have been what it may, yet when once it can plead such prescription of time as to have received a fixed and determinate character, it must be assumed to be founded in the consent of the parties, and to be, to all intents and purposes, a compact or covenant, of the same kind with that which lies at the foundation of all human society. The parties are knit together by numerous ties; care and protection are due to the slave, who is bound, in his turn, to render the duty of gratitude and service to the master. The relation can

* Law of Nature and Nations, Book VI., chap. iii., sect. 9.

not be severed at the will of the parties; it has passed beyond their control, and is established by the decree and order of divine Providence. The slave can not in equity fall back on his natural right of freedom; for he must be presumed, by his own consent, to have waived that right for the sake of the life and nurture which he owes under God to his master. He can not justly claim exemption on the ground that a definite portion of his time and labor is an adequate compensation for his early nurture; since the very conditions on which the contract was undertaken, and to which he is presumed to have consented, are perpetual service on the one hand, and perpetual maintenance on the other; and he has the less inducement to make this claim, when it is considered that the contract includes his support in sickness and in old age. Hence the law of Nature, a prime principle of which is fidelity to contracts, enjoins servants to obey their masters in all lawful commands; and Revelation does but expand with greater clearness, and enforce under higher sanctions, the law which Nature imposes, when it commands servants to be subject to their masters. It is the same here as in other compacts: nothing can justify failure of duty on the part of the slave but the abuse of his right on the part of the master. Oppression and cruelty on the part of the master may justify, as they are pretty sure to cause, desertion or revolt on the part of the slave. But the case is exceptional; and hence the scriptures enjoin submission in this as well as in the case of children and other subjects of legitimate authority, without limitation or reserve: "Servants, obey your masters;" "Children, obey your parents;" and, "Let every soul be subject to the higher powers; for there is no power but of God."

It may be said that American slavery originated neither in the wants of society, nor in legitimate warfare, but that it began in piracy and robbery, and was introduced under circumstances of aggravated cruelty. Be it so. I see no occasion to investigate its origin, and have certainly no disposition to defend it. For, in spite of the ingenious pleas of Mr. Dunning * and all its apologists, I believe the way in which African slavery was introduced into this country to be the foulest of all blots on human nature; the most baneful fruit of that *accursed greed of gold* † which sucks its poisonous nutriment from baseness and cruelty, and from all the meanest and boldest vices under heaven.

Be the guilt on the heads of its authors! It does not affect the American people who have declared the slave-trade to be piracy: it does not stain the slavery that now exists under the laws of our Southern States; it does not touch, in the slightest degree, the relation of master and slave as it now exists on the American soil. For the relation which now ties the Southern master to

* See his argument in the Somerset case, as given in Loft's Reports.

† Sacra auri fames.

his slaves is formed with those who are born under his own roof, or on his own domain, and not with their African progenitors. It is a personal relation; and like all other personal relations, derives its moral quality from the parties that directly form and sustain it, and from no others; and is either right or wrong in virtue of acts that have passed between the persons directly united in it, and not in virtue of acts that transpired before they were born; and for which, therefore, they can not, in the nature of things, be in the least degree responsible. The rape of the Sabines was no derogation to the peaceful and honorable marriages that followed it in the settled times of the Roman republic; and as little can the violence in which slavery originated in any wise taint or corrupt the relation that naturally grows up between a master and the slaves born in his house and nurtured by his care. And England, for it is servility to English opinion which has generated this Northern hatred of Southern institutions; England, I say, should learn to discriminate between the slavery which was introduced by violence and piracy into our colonies under her patronage, and the peaceful and orderly institution which has grown up under the shadow of our laws since our own self-respect moved us to withdraw from her jurisdiction.

For the relation, however it may have originated, involving, as it now does in our Southern States, mutual obligations, and knitting together innocent parties in sacred ties, manifestly rests less on the will of men, than on the appointment of God, "in whom is no injustice, and who alone knoweth best how to proportion His punishment unto men's offenses;" and we might as reasonably call on the New Englanders to restore their country to the ghosts of the aboriginal Indians, whom their fathers drove out of it, or on the United States to return to their subjection to Great Britain, as to deny the right of the Southern planter to the labor of his slaves because their progenitors some two hundred years ago were abducted from Africa. Why can not men understand that there is a Providence which governs the world, as well as a God that created it, and that, while they reject the appointments of God, they are on the high-road to the denial of His being? It is the fact of slavery, the now established relation of master and servant, and not the origin of that relation, with which we of this generation are concerned. If the relation be innocent in itself, we are under no moral obligation to abrogate it; if it be productive of mutual benefits which could not be so well obtained without it, it would be folly to abolish it; if it involve, as it clearly does, a sacred, though tacit compact, it would be criminal to neglect the obligations of that contract; and if it be maintained in good faith, and cemented in the bonds of peace and friendship and social order, it is purely diabolical to sow the seeds of alienation and hatred among its subjects, and to seek to overthrow it by violence and bloodshed.

To the theory that slavery rests on the basis of contract, it has been objected; 1, that the slave had no power to transfer to another his natural rights; and, 2, that he receives from his master no competent consideration for his labor; both objections being founded on the nature of contracts, to the existence of which it is necessary that there should be a power to give, a power to receive, and a sufficient consideration.

As to the former: Pray, what *natural rights* does the slave transfer to his master? Right to life? The slave has neither given it, nor does the master pretend to have received it. Right to liberty? The slave, indeed, is presumed to have transferred to the master the use of his bodily liberty, so far as it is necessary in order to that service for life, which he is presumed to have promised and bound himself to render. But has he not the right to do this? Say no, and who, then, deprives him of his *natural right?* You who deny him the right to dispose of his labor for life, because the municipal law would forbid him if he lived at the North, or I who contend that the slave, in virtue of his humanity and in common with all mankind, *has* this right until the State, for the real or fancied good of the *individual*, steps in to restrain him in this right and to forbid its exercise? Or is it the right to the pursuit of happiness, the transfer of which is to annul the contract? But neither has the slave transferred this right; he has merely exchanged, or is justly presumed to have exchanged the pursuit of happiness in the wilds of uncultivated nature for the pursuit of happiness in an humble vocation in civilized and Christian society.

The truth is, that this whole class of objections applies only to the English theory, which supposes slavery to be founded on *force*, and to vest the master with an *absolute* power over his servants. It does not apply to slavery, considered as a peaceable and settled relation of orderly society, and therefore not to American slavery.

The other objection represents the theory of contract as untenable for want of a competent consideration; meaning that the provision made for the slave by the master is not a consideration of sufficient value to constitute a contract. But is this so? What is a competent consideration for the labor of the poor if it be not nurture in infancy, maintenance in health, support in sickness and old age, and a relief from the uncertainty and mental anxieties inseparable from the lot of those who are compelled to provide for themselves? Are our American slaves deprived of this provision? On the contrary, their rights in this respect are secured by the laws of the States in which they live; and it is, I believe, the common testimony of those who have either visited or resided in those States, that the slaves are a happy and contented people. Dr. Lieber himself, certainly no friend to the institution, tells us that "it is generally admitted that the slave is nowhere better treated than in the slaveholding States of this Union;"* and I believe he might have added with truth that slaves are better cared for in our Southern States than the laboring classes of any other country on earth. And the England and New England assailants of the institution, instead of denying the fact when pressed with it, do but ascribe it to the mercenary motives of the master (who provides for his slaves, it is said, on the same principle as for his horses and cattle), and redouble their dismal ululations over the besotted ignorance of the negro, who is content to remain *a slave!*—themselves slaves to *a word!*

The statistical tables tell us that the blacks of New England increased six *per cent.* in ten years, while those of the Slave States increased twenty-six *per cent.* in the same time; which, allowing a large margin for the influence of climate, and for the number of free blacks in the South, still leaves us pretty fair ground to conclude that the slaves, on the whole, have no reason to complain of insufficient compensation. Besides, if they are not well paid for their labor, how shall we explain the fact, insisted on by our political economists, that slave labor is more unproductive than free labor? For what does this mean, if it be not that the negroes, while slaves, get more comforts in proportion to the amount of work they perform, than they would get if they were free? And, once more, if our American slaves are not

* *Encyclopedia Americana.* Art., *Slavery.*

contented with their condition, how shall we explain the fact, attested by a hundred witnesses, of their fidelity and attachment to their masters? How account for the notorious failure of the abolitionists, after thirty years of diabolical agitation, to excite them to an insurrection? A number of fugitives, not more in proportion to the millions of slaves than are the women who claim men's rights in the North, in proportion to the myriads who are content to shine in the proper virtues of their sex, are about all they have accomplished in the way of liberation.

Do you say that the slave works on compulsion and from fear of the lash, and that, therefore, slavery can not rest on moral grounds, but is upheld by violence? I repeat, that facts are, as a general rule, against this view of the case. Southern men, men who are on the spot, who know whereof they affirm, and are incapable of misrepresentation, tell us, almost with one voice, that their slaves, as a general rule, love their masters and are beloved by them; and that they are contented and happy, except so far as they are inspired with hatred, made discontented with their lot, and turned into fiends by anti-slavery agitators. Citizens of our Northern States, who have visited and resided at the South, bear testimony by hundreds to the same facts. Nay, the abolitionists themselves confirm the facts; for, instead of disproving them, they twist them into a proof of the degradation of the slave, who must be free according to their notions of freedom, or else his contentment in servitude is a proof of his abject and miserable condition! So they dispose of general statements on the one side of the question. But particular and exceptional cases on the other side, how eagerly do they press them into proofs of wholesale oppression and violence! "Contract!" methinks I hear them exclaim; "look at the poor fugitive from his master's service! He bound by contract! A good joke, truly." But ask these same men what binds *them* to society? Are they slaves to their rulers? O, no! They are bound together by the COMPACT on which society is founded. Very good; but did you ever sign this compact? Did your fathers ever sign it? "No; it is a tacit and implied compact." Good again! But some there are who break this compact; who turn vagrants, robbers, murderers; and you take them and shut them up in your poor-houses, jails, and state-prisons or you hang them on a gallows. Does this prove the social compact a nullity? or that the people are not obliged by such compact to be subject to civil government? Not at all; it only proves that a few unprincipled and ungovernable men, who have violated the compact, have received their deserts. And yet, though the great body of masters and slaves are, in fact, tied to each other by the like tacit and implied compact, you cite the case of a runaway slave as a proof that there *is* no such compact, and that slavery is upheld only by violence.

It is the same compact, with the addition of certain formalities that make it express, instead of leaving it to be tacit and implied, which supplies our army and navy with labor, our commercial marine, and mechanical factories. Insubordinates in the army and navy are flogged; insurgents and deserters are shot; the master mechanic may seize his fugitive apprentice and throw him into the nearest jail; and the merchant, though he can not seize the sailors that abscond from their captain in a foreign port, will yet denounce, in no measured terms, their rascality in breaking their engagements, deserting their vessel, and depriving the owners of the profits of the voyage. Not a word of complaint have we in these cases of the want of justice and equity in holding men to their contracts (made perhaps in an unguarded moment), at the expense of their comfort and lives; not a thought of sympathy for the deserter that is shot, or the apprentice that is imprisoned, or the sailor that is denounced and not punished only because he can not be caught; but show us a fugitive slave, and forthwith the community is in a blaze; his obligations to his master, or his possible delinquencies are not thought of; but, in the name of liberty, humanity, and justice, men are summoned to his rescue! Neither the soldier, nor the seaman, nor the apprentice, but only the colored gentleman from the South, may honorably repudiate his obligation to labor. Verily, we live in "an age of progress."

With these evidences before me that the slaves do receive a competent consideration for their labor, I hope I may be allowed, under the lead of publicists of the greatest name, to regard slavery as resting on contract; and to believe, moreover, that under this contract for life, which neither master nor slave can, as a general rule, escape, but which is bound on them both, by the providence of Almighty God, the slave does infinitely better for himself than he would do if he were left to make contracts for himself, without a master, and, from time to time, as his humor might move him, or his natural indolence allow. Nay, more; I believe that the slaves themselves are sensible that the contract now tacitly subsisting between them and their masters is to their own advantage; for it is inconceivable to my mind that four millions of human creatures would, in spite of the incessant efforts of abolition emissaries, for the last thirty years, to excite them to rebellion, remain in servitude, unless they were content to remain in it; and this feeling of child-like contentment (for these slaves are but children in mind), could it assume the shape of intellectual expression, and be translated into the language of educated minds, would be a plain confession that God, by raising up for them humane and considerate masters, had made a better provision for them than they could have made for themselves.

Since the abolition of slavery in our Northern States a new generation has arisen, who know nothing of its actual working, and are apt to take their notions of it from works of fiction. We who are old enough to remember this sort of servitude, however thankfully we may acquiesce in the wisdom which, by abolishing it, has added to the comfort of the rich, in proportion as it lessened their responsibility for the poor, know that slaves were not all either oppressed, or despised, or discontented with their lot. I myself have known slaves (at the North, I mean; for, with the exception of one very brief and melancholy visit in Virginia, I have never been south of the dividing line) who were an honor to human nature; who justly appreciated their condition, and were content and happy in the discharge of its duties; and it may, perchance, be a relief to the reader, after the perusal of a tedious chapter, if I give him the history of one such. It is the case of Cane, who was a slave in the possession of Major H., of Long Island—a man, much respected in his day, but for many years deceased.

Cane was a man; intelligent, honest, and trustworthy; with a certain dignity of demeanor, relieved by a vein of comic humor. He well knew, though he had never learned it from Plautus:

> Simul flare sorbereque haud facile
> Est; ego hic esse et illic simul haud posse;

that he could not suck and whistle in the same breath;

could not at the same time enjoy his freedom and his claim on his master for support; and of the two he had sense enough to see that the latter was more suited to his capacity and condition. When the time which the law had prescribed for the limit of slavery had expired. and the hour of emancipation had come, the Major took Cane aside, and a dialogue to the following effect took place between them. I give it from memory, and substantially as it was told me by a grandson of Major H., who, then a boy, was present, and heard it:

Major H.—"Well, Cane, the day has arrived, which the law has set for the termination of your slavery; and I have called you to tell you that you are now a free man."

C.—"Sorry for it, master."

Major H.—"What, Cane! sorry to be free?"

C.—"Well, master, Cane has always been free enough to look after master's business, and to mind his own; and that is all the freedom Cane wants."

Major H.—"Well, but, Cane, you will have that freedom now. You are an industrious man, and can work, and be paid for your labor. There are many persons that will be glad to employ you."

C.—"Sorry to leave old master."

Major H.—"Why, for that matter, Cane, you need not leave me. You may continue to work for me as you have done, and I will pay you your wages at the end of every month."

C.—"That will not suit Cane, master."

Major H.—"Why not, Cane?"

C.—"Well, master, suppose Cane takes sick, or grows old, what is to become of him?"

Major H.—"That 's right, Cane; look out for a rainy day; but the way to provide for that is to save your money."

C.—"What does Cane know about money? He has no place to keep it. Suppose, he saves it, and takes it to Master S. or Master J. to keep for him; and, before the rainy day comes, Master S. or Master J. blows up, and goes to smash; how will Cane get his money then? Tell me that, master."

Major H.—"True, Cane, such a thing might happen, but——"

C.—"But I tell you, master, what might not happen, and that is that while I work for old master, I should not always find a good home in old master's house. That is the best bank for Cane's money."

Major H.—"Well, then, Cane, you wish to stay and work on the farm, and live with me all the same as if the law had never given you your freedom?"

C.—"That 's what I *should* like, if it had not been for this law. But now, suppose master dies first? If master will promise that Cain shall always live in his family, then Cain will promise always to work in his family."

"So be it, Cane," was his master's response; and so it was. Cain continued to live in his master's family for the remainder of his days, ashamed neither of the condition nor of the name of slave. On the contrary, he had little respect for the free blacks, and several amusing colloquies which he had with them are still remembered. It was Cane's fixed opinion that the negroes needed the protection of the whites, and were not competent to take care of themselves. "I am sure I am not," he would say, "and I think myself equal to the best of them." And before the days of emancipation dawned, if Cane caught a straggler whom he suspected of being a runaway slave, he was pretty sure to lock him up in the barn till his master came to claim him, and never suffered him to depart without some wholesome advice on the duties of his station, and the misery of being, to use his own words, "a poor, shivering, starving free negro."

Though a faithful and industrious creature, Cain was sadly profane, and as neglectful of religious duties as any man of fashion. But time brought its changes. He lived to be old and infirm, and under the sadness of old age, became serious and thoughtful of the future world. The same kindness which supplied his temporal wants in health, ministered to his spiritual wants in sickness and old age. Some member of the family daily read to him, at his own request, a portion of the Holy Scriptures. He died beloved by them all, and was buried in the family ground, where a monument is still to be seen with the following inscription to his memory:

"Beneath this stone was put
The mortal part of CANE, a colored person:
He was born 27th of December, 1738,
And died the 12th of January, 1814;
In the 77th year of his age.

Cane was an honest man.
Tho' nature tinged his skin, and custom marked him slave,
His mind was free and independent.
His life all through was such as did command
Esteem from those who loved him;
And in death he showed examples of Religion
Full (of proofs) convincing of his Christian faith
THAT HIS REDEEMER LIVED AND HE SHOULD SEE HIS FACE.
'Act well thy part; there all the honor lies.'"

CHAPTER XI.

ANGLICAN THEORY OF SLAVERY.

FROM what has been said, it evidently appears that slavery, when founded on mutual consent and productive of mutual benefit, is agreeable to the law of Nature. Not that the law of Nature creates the relation of master and slave any more than it creates other social relations, but that when the relation is once formed, the law of Nature requires its faithful observance and forbids its violent dissolution. Just as the law of Nature does not oblige a man to marry and to have children, but on the supposition that he is a father, obliges him and his children to the reciprocal duties growing out of their mutual relation; or as it does not oblige men to form contracts and to hold real estate, yet when contracts are formed and the distinctions of property are defined, it does oblige them to keep their engagements and to refrain from trespassing on their neighbors' premises; so, though the law of Nature does not oblige some men to be masters and others to be slaves, yet when once the compact is formed and the relation fairly established, the law of Nature clearly ratifies the compact and regulates the relation that grows out of it. It binds the parties together with the ties of a moral union; it enjoins on both reciprocal duties; it forbids the master to withhold care and protection from the slave, and the slave to withhold fealty and service from the master. The law itself is immutable and becomes operative as soon as occasion arises for its use and application.

But there is another condition of life which is also called slavery, but which is very unlike the former, and indeed has nothing in common with it except the name, and which, yet, chiefly from the force of language, is often confounded with it. This condition of life, for I can not call it a condition of human society, is upheld by force, and supposes master and slave to be joined together by none of the common ties and offices of humanity, but to live in a constant state of war and enmity. The consideration of this unhappy relation is proper to the law of Nations, in the treatises on which it occupies a large space, and is not otherwise connected with the law of Nature than as this law is appealed to in support of the principles on which the law of Nations is founded.

For the better satisfaction of the reader I shall describe this sort of slavery in the words of others.

Having remarked that "it is not repugnant to natural law, that slavery may be derived from some personal act," *i. e.*, from some *voluntary agreement* or for some *crime*, and having treated of both these species of slavery, in his first and second book, in connection with the law of Nature, Grotius, in the third book of his treatise (*De Jure Belli et Pacis*), and in the seventh chapter (entitled "Of the Right over Prisoners"), proceeds as follows:

"But by the law of Nations (which I am now treating of) slavery is of a more large extent, both as to persons and effects. For if we consider the persons, not only they who surrender themselves, or engage by promise to do it, are reputed slaves, but all persons whatsoever, taken in a solemn war, as soon as they shall be brought within our garrisons, as Pomponius tells us."

Grotius next quotes several authorities to show that captives in solemn wars, whatever may have been their previous standing, were anciently regarded as the slaves of the conqueror; that both they and their children (after their captivity) were accounted his absolute property,—to be put to death, sold into bondage, or otherwise disposed of at his will. He then adds:

"But the effects of this right are infinite, so that there is nothing that the lord (or master) may not do to his slave; as Seneca the father said, no torment but what may be inflicted on him with impunity, nothing commanded him, but what may be exacted with the utmost rigor and severity; so that all manner of cruelty may be exercised by the lords (masters) on their slaves; but that this license is somewhat restrained by the civil law. 'It is generally allowed by all nations to the lord (master) to have power of life and death over his slave,' we are told by Caius the lawyer. He also adds that this large power had been limited by the Roman laws in their own territories. Hither we may refer that of Donatus to Terentius, 'What may not a lord (master) lawfully do to his slave?' "

Here follow two short paragraphs, not relevant to my present purpose; after which, Grotius adds:

"Now this large power is granted by the law of Nations for no other reason than that the captors, being tempted by so many advantages, might be inclined to forbear that utmost rigor allowed them by the law of killing their prisoners, either in the fight, or in cold blood. As I said before, the name of *servants* (Pomponius tells us) arose from this, that generals sold their prisoners, thereby preserving them from death. I said that they might be inclined to forbear; for there is no argument to engage them to it, if we respect this law of Nations, but a motive drawn from interest."

We have reason to be thankful that the law of Nations, as understood and acknowledged among modern and civilized peoples, forbids the putting of prisoners to death, except they have committed some crime worthy of death, and that the humane and salutary customs which have been introduced for the alleviation of the evils of war (such as exchange of prisoners, releasing them on parole, etc.), have cut off all pretexts for the barbarous practice. But this does not affect the point in hand, which is to show that the right of the master over the slave was anciently derived from the law of Nations, and was made by that law to include an *absolute* power over the slave; and that this right of dominion was acknowledged at Rome, and among all nations (see the above quotation from Caius the lawyer), except in so far as it was restrained and limited by the civil law.

Here, then, we have two conditions of life, *essentially* distinct from each other, and yet both denominated *slavery*. The one confers a right of dominion derived from the law of Nature, which is immutable and everywhere the same, and of necessity subject to the limitations of this law, which allows nothing contrary to justice; while the other confers a right of dominion, derived from the law of Nations, which is mutable, and in fact now revokes the right which it once conferred; and a right, moreover, which is absolute, and authorizes the master to inflict on his slave all sorts of cruelties which the law of the State does not specifically forbid.

This sort of slavery, founded on the right of conquest, and upheld merely by force, formerly existed, as in all the nations of Europe, so also in Great Britain. It has long since died out in fact, but it is still this, and nothing else than this, which the English people mean by the word *slavery*. I have before alluded to the following passage of Mr. Locke, and now beg the reader's perusal of it entire:

"Freedom from absolute, arbitrary power is so necessary and closely joined with a man's preservation, that he can not part with it, but by what forfeits his life and preservation together. For a man not having the power of his own life, *can not,* by compact, or his own consent, *enslave himself* to any one, nor put himself under the absolute, arbitrary power of another, to take away his life when he pleases. Nobody can give more power than he has himself; and he that can not take away his own life, can not give another power over it. Indeed, having by his fault forfeited his own life, by some act that deserves death, he to whom he has forfeited it, may (when he has him in his power) delay to take it. For, whenever he finds the hardship outweighs the value of his life, 'tis in his power, by resisting the will of his master, to draw on himself the death he desires.

"This is the perfect condition of slavery, which is nothing else but *the state of war continued between the lawful conqueror and a captive.* For if once *compact* enter between them, and make an agreement for a limited power on the one side, and obedience on the other, *the state of war and slavery* ceases, as long as the compact endures. For, as has been said, no man can, by agreement pass over to another that which he hath not in himself, a power over his own life.

"I confess, we find among the Jews as well as other nations, that men did sell themselves; but it is plain this was only to *drudgery, not to slavery.* For it is evident the person sold was not under an absolute, arbitrary, despotical power. For the master could not have power to kill him at any time, whom, at a certain time he was obliged to let go free out of his service; and the master of such a servant was so far from having an arbitrary power over his life that he could not at pleasure so much as maim him, but the loss of an eye or a tooth set him free." Ex. xxi.*

I have somewhere seen this eminent man charged with inconsistency and a departure from his own principles, because the constitution of the Carolinas, which he drafted, contains provisions in favor of slavery. Probably the inconsistency is merely verbal.

I now ask particular attention to a passage which I shall transcribe from the Leviathan of Hobbes; a man whose principles I detest, but who for clearness and vigor of thought and expression is unsurpassed, I believe, by any author in the English language.

"Dominion acquired by conquest, or victory in war, is that which some writers call DESPOTICAL, from Δεσπότης, which signifieth a *lord*, or *master;* and is the dominion of the master over his servant. And this dominion is then acquired to the victor, when the vanquished, to avoid the present stroke of death, covenanteth, either in express words, or by other sufficient signs of the will, that so long as his life and the liberty of his body is allowed him, the victor shall have the use thereof

* Locke's Works, vol. ii. p. 165.

at his pleasure. And after such covenant made, the vanquished is a SERVANT, and not before; for by the word *servant* (whether it be derived from *servire*, to serve, or from *servare*, to save, which I leave the grammarians to dispute), is not meant a captive which is kept in prison, or bonds, till the owner of him that took, or bought him of him that did, shall consider what to do with him; for such men, commonly called slaves, have no obligation at all, but may break their bonds, or the prison, and kill, or carry away captive their master, justly; but one that being taken, hath corporal liberty allowed him, and upon promise not to run away, nor to do violence to his master, is trusted by him.

"It is not, therefore, the victory that giveth the right of dominion over the vanquished, but his own covenant. Nor is he obliged because he is conquered, that is to say beaten and taken, or put to flight, but because he cometh in and submitteth to the victor. Nor is the victor obliged by an enemy rendering himself (without promise of life), to spare him for this his yielding to discretion, which obliges not the victor longer than in his own discretion he shall think fit.

"And that which men do when they demand (as it is now called) *quarter*, (which the Greeks called Ζωγρία, *taking alive*) is to evade the present fury of the victor by submission, and to compact for their life with ransom, or service; and, therefore, he that hath quarter, hath not his life given, but deferred till further deliberation; for it is not a yielding on condition of life, but to discretion. And then only is his life in security, and his service due, when the victor hath trusted him with his corporal liberty. For slaves that work in prisons, or fetters, do it not of duty, but to avoid the cruelty of their task-masters."*

There are two remarkable positions in this passage which I can not help, in passing, commending to the attention of our modern radicals, (who, or whose progenitors, have drawn from Hobbes many of their detestable maxims) and especially to those of them who have given him the sonorous appellation of "The philosopher of Malmesbury."

The first is that Hobbes concedes to slaves (or servants, as he more accurately calls them) the possession of LIBERTY. The slave (servant), according to him, has, like other men, liberty as well as life; and the precise difference between the slave and the freeman, in this respect, is that the slave, or servant, has, while the freeman has not, transferred *the use* of his liberty to another.

The other is that servitude, or slavery, as we now call it, in its ordinary form, is, according to Hobbes, founded on compact or covenant. The relation of master and servant, even though it originate in conquest, yet, as Hobbes clearly shows, is capable of exchanging, and for

* *Hobbes's Leviathan,* folio, London, A. D. 1651, pp. 103, 104.

the most part actually exchanges, its hostile character for one that is peaceable and friendly. It passes, he says (as indeed it is very apt to pass), from the law of might to the law of right; so that the slave is morally and religiously bound to serve his master, and defrauds him by becoming a fugitive from his service. Strange that Hobbes, the author of the Leviathan, to whose poison Bramhall, Cumberland, and Clarendon, his contemporaries, and the brightest intellects of their age, taxed their energies to furnish an antidote; that Hobbes, a name which has been handed down to execration in Church and State, and which will be execrated as long as the interests of government and religion are united; that Hobbes, I say, should be needed in this age to give lessons in government and religion to Christian statesmen and ministers of the gospel! But so it is; and as I would cheerfully give the father of mischief and all his progeny their due, so I take particular pleasure in adding "the philosopher of Malmesbury!" to the names of Grotius and Puffendorff, and other eminent civilians, who, by resting slavery on the ground of CONTRACT, have helped us to clear the precepts of the gospel, which require slaves to obey their masters, from the imputation of favoring arbitrary power, and to resolve them into the prime principles of reason and nature.

But to return from this digression. The reader will have observed that, as Mr. Locke distinguishes *slavery* from *drudgery*, so Hobbes distinguishes *slavery* from *servitude;* and that both these authors agree in making slavery consist in an unlimited subjection to absolute dominion. The slave, in their sense of the word, is one who holds his life and liberty subject, not to the conditional use, but to the absolute disposal of the master; who, by the right of conquest, and under the law of nations, may at any time, and of his own mere will, deprive him of both; may maim his limbs, or take his life, without being liable to be called to account by any human authority. This sort of slavery, as Hobbes intimates, was common among the Romans; who either could not or would not admit all their captives into a covenant relation, or work them on parole, but confined many of them in their *ergastula,* in prisons and in galleys, and made them work in chains and fetters; not trusting them with any degree of bodily liberty, nor seeking to influence them by higher motives, but governing them solely by fear and cruelty.

It would be easy to fill a volume with extracts from the writings of philosophers and historians, orators and poets, and authors of every class, who use the word slavery in the sense so clearly defined by Hobbes and Mr. Locke. But to what end? Who does not know that this notion of slavery, derived from its most aggravated form among the ancient Romans, has been incorporated in the philosophy, the divinity, the science, the literature, the poetry, and, of late years, in the statesmanship of the British nation? I do not mean that this notion of slavery is peculiar to Great Britain: it prevails to a considerable extent in Europe, and shows itself in European writers. Vattel, for instance, has no other idea of slavery than as "a state contrary to the nature of man," "a continued state of war;" and he rejoices (and every defender of American slavery will cordially and consistently rejoice with him) that "this disgrace of mankind is happily extinct in Europe." But I mean that this notion of slavery prevails in Great Britain to the exclusion almost of every other. Villeinage itself, which formerly existed in England, was an aggravated form of slavery. The villeins (*in gross*) were originally captives at the Conquest; they were compelled to perform the most servile offices; and "both they and their children," says Dr. Harris' Notes on Justinian, "were the absolute property of their lords, who might lease them out to others for years, or for life, or make an absolute sale of them." And slavery in the British West Indies, left to the management of overseers, while the proprietors were absent from their plantations, was, very probably, upheld by terror and cruelty, and had no opportunity of transition into that peaceable and friendly relation, which subsists in our Southern States. In fact, we shall look in vain, if I mistake not, to the jurists of Great Britain, in modern times, for those just and profound views of slavery, considered as a social institution, which have been developed by Grotius, Puffendorf, and other European authors. Our English friends and cousins have no idea of a slavery, which is founded in contract, and which, because it is founded in contract, secures the *natural rights* of the slave. Their traditionary and sole notion of slavery is that of servitude founded on conquest, and upheld only by terror and cruelty.

And this tradition of the English mind has been transmitted to New England, and made the generative cause of all its abolition proclivities. Differing essentially and by unmistakeable features from that form of slavery which exists in our Southern States, and agreeing with it only in name, it is yet put forward persistently and in every variety of form as essentially the same thing; and that just and laudable hatred which every ingenuous mind feels against the one form of servitude is cunningly or ignorantly excited by argument and declamation, and brought to bear upon the other; and the southern planter, surrounded by his attached and affectionate domestics, and resorting to coercion only as an ultimatum for the necessary support of authority (as is done in the army and navy, and indeed in schools and families, and in almost every form of secular government) is held up to the execration of mankind for no better reason, that I can see, than because his servants are called *slaves*, and the poets and philosophers, the Cowpers and Lockes of England have chosen to affix a very horrid meaning to the *name*.

But I have another reason for calling these two descriptions of slavery, the one limited and sanctioned by the law of Nature, the other unlimited and supported only by an exploded *dictum* of the law of Nations; I say, I have another reason for calling the one *American* and the other *British;* and that is, that the government of the United States, by its highest public functionaries, has solemnly, and in the face of the world, recognized and declared the slavery of our Southern States to be of the former description, and has disallowed and repelled the assumption of the British government referring it to the latter description. To explain my meaning:

It has often happened that coasting vessels, under the jurisdiction of the United States, having slaves on board, either as hands or as servants, attending their owners, or for the purpose of being carried from port to port, have been driven by stress of weather or other necessity, to take refuge in harbors belonging to some of the British dependencies of America; and that in some such cases, the slaves, owned by citizens of the United States, have been set free by the authorities of the place. The *Creole* was an example of this kind. This vessel, having slaves on board, was taken, in consequence of a mutiny, into a port of the British dominions, and the slaves, as was alleged, were liberated by the interference of the local authorities.

In a letter, dated August 1, 1842, Mr. Webster, at that time Secretary of State for the United States, brought the case of the *Creole* to the attention of Lord

Ashburton, then residing at Washington, and clothed with general powers by the British government to act in its behalf in the adjustment of the disputes that were pending between the two governments. In this document Mr. Webster does not confine himself to the particular case of the *Creole*, but goes at length into the subject, and affirms generally the right of the United States to exact compensation of the British government in behalf of American proprietors, whose slaves have been set at liberty in the manner above indicated. In the course of his argument, Mr. Webster remarks:

"If a vessel be driven by weather into the ports of another nation, it would hardly be alleged by any one that, by the mere force of such arrival within the waters of the State, the law of that State would so attach to the vessel as to affect existing rights of property between persons on board, whether arising from contract or otherwise. The local law would not operate to make the goods of one man to become the goods of another man. Nor ought it to affect their personal obligations or existing relations between themselves; nor was it ever supposed to have such effect until the delicate and exciting question which has caused these interferences in the British islands arose. The local law in these cases dissolves no obligations or relations lawfully entered into or lawfully existing according to the laws of the ship's country. If it did, intercourse of civilized men between nation and nation must cease. Marriages are frequently celebrated in one country in a manner not lawful or valid in another; but did anybody ever doubt that marriages are valid all over the civilized world, if valid in the country in which they took place? Did any one ever imagine that local law acted upon such marriages to annihilate their obligation, if the party should visit a country in which marriages must be celebrated in another form?

"It may be said that, in such instances, personal relations are founded in contract, and therefore to be respected; but that the relation of master and slave is not founded in contract, and therefore is to be respected only by the law of the place which recognizes it. Whoever so reasons, encounters the authority of the whole body of public law, from Grotius down; because there are numerous instances in which the law itself presumes or implies contracts; and prominent among those instances is the very relation which we are now considering, and which relation is holden by law to draw after it mutuality of obligation." *

Personal relations that are founded in universal justice, are worthy of universal respect; but personal relations which are founded in injustice, and are upheld in opposition to natural justice, by the laws of a particular country, have no claim to respect outside of that country. In demanding, therefore, that the relation of

* See Correspondence with Lord Ashburton, Webster's Works, vol. vi., pp. 303–318.

master and slave, both belonging to the United States, and continuing within the jurisdiction of the same, should be respected in British ports, Mr. Webster was sure to be met with the objection, that this relation is not a just and social relation, like that of husband and wife, parent and child, but one which exists in opposition to universal justice, and only in virtue of local laws; which, in the case under consideration, are the laws of some one of the United States, and the guaranty of the Federal Government; and that the relation consequently expires when its subjects pass beyond the limits within which those laws are operative, and to which that guarantee extends. For example, if a citizen of New York is traveling with his minor child, or if a master with his apprentice is traveling in a foreign country, and in company with him is a citizen of South Carolina, with his slave; it would be accounted barbarous in the authorities of that country to interfere with the father in the government of his child, or with the master in the government of his apprentice, because these relations are consistent with natural justice, and entitled to universal respect. On the other hand, it would be no violation of the comity of nations, but an evidence of high civilization, if the authorities of the same country interfered in order to effect the enfranchisement of the slave, because the relation of master and slave is repugnant to natural justice, and ceases to exist when it passes beyond the protection of positive law. This I understand to be the objection; and I wish to fix the reader's attention on Mr. Webster's answer to the objection. Mr. Webster, as the reader will have observed, takes the ground that the relation of master and slave is *not* repugnant to natural justice, but that it is founded in *contract*, and involves mutual obligations; and he declares distinctly and boldly, and under the high responsibility of his exalted station, that whoever takes the opposite ground—whoever denies that slavery is founded in contract, and is consonant to natural justice—"ENCOUNTERS THE WHOLE BODY OF PUBLIC LAW FROM GROTIUS DOWN!" Of course this declaration of Mr. Webster, or rather of the President of the United States through him, does not apply to slavery universally: it does not apply to slavery as it *may* exist by the law of Nations; nor to the slavery of barbarous countries, where captives are, for no personal crimes, totally deprived of bodily liberty, and subjected to unmerciful treatment: but it is limited, by the occasion on which it was made, to that form of slavery which exists in our Southern States, under the guaranty of the Constitution of the United States; and so understood and limited, the declaration, I believe, can never be successfully impugned.*

* A legal friend, who first directed my attention to the above quoted letter of Mr. W., adds the following:

"In the speech delivered by Mr. Webster, in defense of the treaty of Washington, in the United States Senate, 6th and 7th April, 1846, he says, 'I refer to the letter to Lord Ashburton on this subject (the

Now, mark the consequence. It is impossible to regard a man as a party to a contract, without regarding him at the same time as possessed of his natural rights as a member of human society, and as having a definite *status* under the government which protects that contract. The United States, therefore, until they repudiate the doctrine which Mr. Webster promulgated in their name, are committed to the recognition of slavery (in those States in which it exists) as a SOCIAL INSTITUTION, and not as a monster that is at war with human society, and refuses to coalesce with the elements of good order; they are committed to the recognition of slaves (in the several States in which they exist) as persons capable of contract, and actually, or at least, impliedly bound by contract, and therefore possessed of those natural rights and faculties without which, no creature can be, either expressly or by implication, a party to a contract; and they are committed, moreover, to the recognition of the relation of master and slave as legitimate by the law of Nature, and entitled, as well (I say not in the same degree) as that of husband and wife, or of father and child, to universal respect. This is American slavery.

Lord Ashburton, in his reply to Mr. Webster, confesses that the American secretary has "advanced some propositions which rather surprise and startle" him: his lordship, however, does "not pretend to judge them,"

Creole case) 'as containing what the *American government* regarded as the true principle of the maritime law.'"

but refers Mr. Webster to London for their discussion. What ground the British government ultimately took in this particular I do not know, and it is needless to inquire; for the temper and opinions of the British public (to *follow which* has become the genius of the English government, and the hard necessity of the English Church), point to the conclusion, in opposition to Mr. Webster and "the whole body of public law," that the slavery existing in our Southern States is not founded in contract; that it is repugnant to natural justice; that the bond which unites master and slave derives its whole strength from local laws, and dissolves of its own accord when it passes beyond the reach of those laws; and that the slave, under the laws of a country that tolerates slavery, has no natural rights, but is a *mere* chattel of his master, distinguished from his inanimate chattels by a principle of vitality, and from his cows and horses by the possession of a human form and figure. This view of slavery seems to be indigenous to the British soil, and therefore I call it the British view, and am willing to accord to the British people whatever glory it may reflect on them. How the clergy of the English Establishment, consistently with such a theory, would reconcile the precepts of the gospel, inculcating obedience to masters, with the dictates of universal reason; or how they would refute the principles of the abolitionists, while resisting (as I believe they would resist) the application of those principles to practice, I am unable to say. If they were compelled to attempt a practical solution of the problem, they would be driven, I apprehend, either to surrender their theory, or to inculcate principles of duty too ethereal for the grasp of English sense, and too sublimated for English practice. However this be, though no man rates, or can rate, more highly than I do, the obligations of our people to their mother country, I have yet felt at liberty to investigate this subject without the bias of English authority; and I am happy that the result of the investigation enables me to take, with a deep conviction of its truth, the ground which my country has in a manner prescribed; to regard the slavery existing in our Southern States as resting on contract, and to regard the relation of master and slave as no cause of shame or reproach, but as entitled to respect, both at home and abroad; as entitled to respect, because legitimate, not only by the laws of the particular States which uphold it, and by the Constitution of the United States, which guaranties its protection, but also by the principles of universal justice; that is, by the LAW OF GOD. And I can not but indulge the hope that the avowal of this sentiment, however it may at first "startle and surprise," will in the end approve itself to the more sober and judicious members of the Anglican Church.

CHAPTER XII.

LIMITATIONS OF AUTHORITY.

BISHOP CUMBERLAND, than whom, in his "*De Legibus Naturæ*,"* no author has searched more deeply into the foundations of society, virtue, and religion, in the course of his chapter "On the original of Dominion and the Moral Virtues," makes the following observation:

"Before I had universally and distinctly considered the original of *all* dominion and right whatsoever, I used, indeed, as most others do, to deduce the Divine dominion entirely from His (God's) being the Creator; for I thought it self-evident that every one was lord of his own powers, which are little different from the *essence* of anything, and that therefore any effect must be subject to him, from whose powers it received its whole essence, as is the case in creation, by which the whole substance of the thing is produced into being.

"But because all *dominion* supposes some *right*, and

* The work, published in the seventeenth century, was translated by Mr. Maxwell, a Prebendary of the Church of Ireland, and printed (with several dissertations of his own) at London, A. D. 1727. The above quotation is from Mr. Maxwell's translation.

all right is a power granted or permitted by some *law*, at least analogically such; therefore, the law granting or permitting dominion, ought *first* to be acknowledged. But law there is none prior to the *natural* law, or that dictate of the Divine wisdom, concerning the best end and the means thereto necessary, which is perfectly agreeable to the law of Nature, and may analogically be called the LAW OF THE DIVINE ACTIONS; I therefore came to this conclusion: That the dominion of God is a right or power given Him by His own wisdom or goodness, as by a law, for the government of all those things which ever have been, or shall be created by Him. In the Divine wisdom is necessarily contained a dictate to pursue the best end by the necessary means; and in the goodness or perfection of the Divine will is, by a like necessity, included a ready consent to promote the same; and these, by a natural analogy, answer to a ratification of this eternal law, whence the divine dominion may take its original."

If, then, God's right to dominion is derived, not from His irresistible power, but from His infinite wisdom and goodness, which serve after the manner of a law to direct the operation of His infinite power; evident it is, that mere power confers on no human creature the right of dominion, and that no one man has the right to govern another otherwise than agreeably to those laws which our Creator has given for the government of all men. Absolute dominion, or the power to direct and dispose of persons and things without regard to justice and equity, which are for us men the surest expressions of the Divine wisdom and goodness, is an attribute neither of God nor of good men, and is coveted only by that pride and selfishness which are the origin of evil and the eternal torment of the wicked.

Whatever rights, then, accrue to us under the law of Nature, are limited by the law of Nature, which commands us to render to all their dues, and restrains us in every relation of life, and in all our actions, from injustice, cruelty, and oppression. The law of Nature, for example, gives the husband authority to govern his wife, but it does not permit him to treat her harshly or cruelly; it gives the father authority over his children, but not to maltreat and abuse them; in neither case is the authority absolute, but in both cases it is limited and restrained to the ends for which it is given by the very law which creates it. So with the relation of master and slave: the law of Nature gives the master authority to govern his slave, but not to abuse him: it limits the exercise of his authority by a just regard to the end for which it is conferred; that is, to render the slave obedient to his just demands, and to obtain from him that service which is the master's due. All beyond this is usurpation and cruelty—abhorrent to the law of Nature.

In truth the law of Nature, in requiring us *to love God supremely, and our neighbor as ourselves* (and this is seen to be the sum and substance of the law of

Nature when *revealed* to us in its full dimensions), imposes an immutable limitation to all the authority it confers; and a limitation which would be as effectual as immutable, if the precept imposing it were duly consulted. Unhappily, however, the very precept which is designed by God to limit authority is used by the perversity of man to subvert and destroy it; being made a pretext for annihilating the distinctions of rank and property in society; and consequently of obliterating the moral virtues of temperance and frugality, benevolence and modesty, which, without these distinctions, would have no scope for exercise, and, indeed, no possibility of existence. But the love or benevolence enjoined by the divine law is no such leveling principle. It requires us to do good offices to all men in their various relations, and in such manner and degree as is best fitted to fulfill the ends of those relations. Hence it can not, in its due exercise, subvert the authority which God has entrusted to any man; but it serves to temper authority, to whomsoever entrusted, and to direct it to the fulfillment of its legitimate end. We admit this in other relations; why not also in that which is under consideration? A man's love for his wife does not require him to abjure his authority over her, but so to exercise it as to attach her to himself, and to make her the trusting and trusted partner of his life. A father's love to his children does not require him to renounce his authority over them, but so to exercise his authority as to fit them for their destined stations in life. A ruler's love for his subjects does not require him to change places with them, but so to govern them as he, if a subject and an honest and upright man, would desire to be governed himself. The love of a judge for a criminal at the bar does not require him to divest himself of his office, or to violate its duties, but it requires him so to exercise his authority as to show all possible kindness and clemency to the accused, consistent with the paramount purpose of giving effect to the just and humane intention of the law. A rich man's love for his poor neighbors does not require him to beggar himself, but so to use his riches as to relieve their necessities. All these things are so nearly self-evident that they scarcely admit of proof, and are commonly received without it. Why, then, should the relation we are considering be counted an exception? Why imagine that love, which is the principle of universal attraction in the moral world, and binds men together in every other just relation of life, should in this relation alone become a principle of repulsion which must of necessity rend them asunder? Surely, unless we are determined to violate all principle and all analogy, we must acknowledge that the love of the master for his slaves does not require him to raise them to the same state of freedom with himself, but that it serves to temper his authority over them, and to direct the exercise of it to the end for which it is given; *i. e.*, to make them faithful and affectionate servants.

It is in this law of universal benevolence, which, as imperfectly and in its rude outlines apprehended by reason, requires us to abstain from injury and to do justice to all men, and which, when revealed to us in its full proportions by its divine Author, becomes the charity of the gospel, requiring us not only to be just, but full of mercy and compassion; it is, I say, in this law that we find the limitation of all human authority. It is by this law that the master (as well as the father and all others invested with authority) is taught and directed, not only to do justice to those under him, but to render them, as far as he can, comfortable and happy in the relations which they hold to him. He is bound to regard them as his fellow-creatures, remembering that the difference between himself and them is not a difference of nature, but of fortune; that he is made of the same clay with them, and that they are made in the same image of God with him; that his authority is but a brief trust for the just and equitable use of which he must account to his Master in heaven. They are his servants, and he has the right to exact of them the service which is his due; but he has no right to overtask them, nor, indeed, to require of them any greater labor than is conducive to his and their mutual benefit, regard being had to their different stations in life. They are part of his family, and he has therefore the right to govern them without accounting to the State, except for such inordinate abuses as its laws prohibit; but he has no right (by the law of Nature, I mean, which restrains us all within much narrower limits than the law of the land) to punish them except for just cause, for their indolence and other faults and vices, and in no other kind or greater degree than is necessary to their amendment. He has a right to the use of their bodily liberty (for how else could he command their service?), but he has no right to require of them anything impossible in Nature or unlawful in morals. The relation in which he stands to them is not inalienable by Nature, like that of parent and child, nor indissoluble by the law of God, natural or positive, like that of husband and wife, but is superinduced on him by Providence, with their implied consent, and may be alienated and dissolved, but not capriciously or wantonly. Strictly speaking, the master has a right only to the service of the slave; and there is evidently nothing in the nature of this right to prevent its transfer to another with the slave's consent, either expressed or gathered, in cases of incapacity, by reasonable implication. Reason, too, allows the transfer, in cases of necessity, arising either from the master's misfortunes or from the incurable vice and obstinacy of the slave, which requires his dismissal from his master's service. All beyond this, if justifiable at all, must be justified, I apprehend, not by the law of Nature, but only by the laws of the land.

To say that this authority is always exercised within the limits which the law of Nature prescribes, would be to affirm of the master more than can be affirmed of any class of men invested with authority in the body politic, in the family, or in other associations involving the governmental relation. Magistrates, husbands, and fathers, clergymen, teachers, masters, or employers, as we now call them, are all liable to the charge of cruel and capricious conduct toward their subordinates. What good reason have we to believe that the proprietor of slaves abuses his trust more than others? His authority is in some respects analogous to that of the father over his children; and although it is not restrained by the sentiment of paternal affection, yet it is restrained by that sentiment of kindliness which is implanted in every human bosom, and by that dictate of our common humanity which excites every man's solicitude in behalf of all those who are dependent on him, and look to him for protection. What reason have we to believe that our Southern brethren are the only men on earth on whom these sentiments are inoperative? And if these motives are less efficacious than the sympathies created by closer ties, may not their defects be compensated by that principle of self-interest which, in the present state of our nature, is more stringent and steady in its operation than any other motive of human action, and which does not, as a general rule, suffer the master to neglect the welfare of his slaves? In this respect, it will be found, I apprehend, that the good providence of God, by infusing seeds of attachment, and by an interweaving of interests among those who, however different in station, are under his common charge, and the objects of his common bounty, but has acted the part of a kind philanthropist, and a wise economist.

In another respect, the authority of the master is analogous to that of the magistrate: he is obliged to punish his slaves for numerous offenses, which in free States can be taken cognizance of only by the magistrate. I would not underrate the advantages that are derived from the formalities of law, and the safeguards with which they surround the liberty, reputation, and property of the humblest citizen. But are the advantages all one side? Is nothing to be said in favor of that state of society, in which the great body of the laboring class stands only in a *mediate* relation to the State? Is the master less interested than the magistrate in the prevention of crime? Is he less likely to be lenient and discriminating in his judgments? Has he fewer inducements to make the punishments which he awards answer the true end of punishment, the reformation and improvement of the offender? For my part I shall be more ready to quarrel with arbitrary power at the South when we get rid of jails and state-prisons at the North.

I am not depreciating freedom, nor am I insensible to the advantages which have been conferred on the white population of the North (at the expense of the blacks) by the abolition of slavery. But if there be any redeeming points in that state of society which exists at the South,

I think we can well afford to take them into account and pass them to the credit of our Southern brethren, in the comparisons which we draw between our own condition and theirs.

Besides the motives already mentioned, there are others of a more general nature, which may be presumed to operate beneficially upon the master. He is responsible to his Maker equally with other men: he has a reputation to maintain among his neighbors and acquaintances, and throughout the world; he has a large stake in society, and is proportionately prompted by public spirit to redress abuses, and to introduce salutary reforms; his slaves, moreover, are part of his family, and his agency for their temporal and spiritual welfare, if he be a Christian man, is quickened by the apostolic precept, "If any man provide not for his own, and especially for those of his own house, he hath denied the faith, and is worse than an infidel." If the slaveholder has strong temptations to oppression and cruelty, let us remember that he has strong motives also to resist these temptations. That he, like other men, is often betrayed into excess, is probable; in which case, it may be hoped, he will be honest enough to confess his fault, and not seek to justify himself by an equivocation like that of Browne, the reputed father of the Independents, who (I have the story from one of his contemporaries) when accused of unmercifully beating his wife, defended himself by saying, that he did not beat her as his wife, but as a termagant.*

It is hardly fair to visit the faults of individuals on the class to which they belong, and on the institutions under which they live. I am sure that we at the North would think we had great reason for complaint, if our magistrates, husbands, fathers, and free institutions to boot, were all brought into disgrace because individuals among us abuse their authority. As to punishments for laziness and lighter offenses, I believe, from what I can learn, that there is more flogging done in an old-fashioned English school, than on a well ordered Southern plantation. And I should be glad to know if the lot of the slave would be less degraded and miserable, if he were compelled to labor from fear of starvation, which, if left to himself, he could not avoid, than it is when he is compelled to labor from fear of the lash, which, as a general rule, he can escape if he will? And as to punishments for more serious offenses, are they less severe in kind and degree, less wholesome in their effects, and more expensive to the State, than those which it would be necessary to inflict on the same class of people, if they were emancipated from their masters, brought into

* Ephraim Pagitt, in his account of the Brownists, Chapter 13th, "*Of their equivocating,*" gives this, among other instances: "And old father Browne, being reproved for beating his old wife, distinguished, that he did not beat her as his wife, but as a curst old woman." HERESIOGRAPHY, *or a description of the Heretics and Sectaries sprung up in these latter times.* London, A. D. 1648.

immediate relation with society, tried by judge and jury, sent for a while to jails and state-prisons, to be thrown back upon the community, greater vagabonds than before? These, as it seems to me, are the true points of comparison, though they are such as novelists and declaimers against slavery find it convenient to overlook.

We are very apt, at the North, to estimate the character of Southern masters from the laws of their respective States, and to impute to them, as a class, those abuses of authority which the laws do not forbid. Nothing can be more manifestly or flagrantly unjust. What would the father of a family, in a free State, think of those who should impute to him every act of tyranny and cruelty which the laws of his State do not forbid him to exercise? And so with persons in other relations. The truth is that persons possessed of authority are restrained from its abuse by a sense of humanity, of justice and reputation, and the thousand other benign motives with which Providence has surrounded them in a Christian community, infinitely more than by the laws of the land; which are designed to guard against the most scandalous abuses, and to operate chiefly on ignoble minds. But allowing the objection its due weight, it deserves to be remarked that Southern legislatures have not been so unmindful of their slaves as we of the North are apt to suppose. They acknowledge the rights of slaves, and have already done much, and, if left to themselves, and not hampered by the officiousness of others, will, in the natural course of things, do more to protect them in these rights. On this subject I beg the attention of the reader to the following extract from an essay on the "Slave Laws of the South," by the Hon. J. B. O'Neall, of South Carolina. I quote from the essay as given by De Bow, in his "Industrial Resources," who remarks that the essay, "though based upon the slave system of that State (S. C.), gives a fair idea of the system throughout the entire South":

"Although slaves," says Judge O'Neall, "by the act of 1740, are declared to be chattels personal, yet they are also in our law considered as persons with many rights and liabilities, civil and criminal.

"The right of protection which would belong to a slave, as a human being, is, by the law of slavery, transferred to the master.

"A master may protect the person of his slave from injury, by repelling force with force, or by action, and in some cases by indictment.

"Any injury done to the person of his slave, he may redress by action of trespass *vi et armis*, without laying the injury done, with a *per quod servitium amisit*, and this, even though he may have hired the slave to another.

"By the act of 1821, the murder of a slave is declared to be a felony, without the benefit of clergy; and by the same act, to kill any slave on sudden heat and passion, subjects the offender, on conviction, to a fine not exceeding five hundred dollars, and imprisonment, not exceeding six months.

"To constitute the murder of a slave, no other ingredients are necessary than such as enter into the offense of murder at common law. So the killing on sudden heat and passion is the same as manslaughter, and a finding by the jury, on an indictment for the murder of a slave, of a killing on sudden heat and passion, is good, and subjects the offender to the punishment of the act; or, on an indictment for the murder of a slave, if the verdict be guilty of manslaughter, it is good, and the offender is to receive judgment under the act.

"An attempt to kill and murder a slave by shooting at him, was held to be a misdemeanor, and indictable as an assault with an intent to kill and murder. This was a consequence of making it murder to kill a slave.

"The act of 1841 makes the *unlawful* whipping or beating of any slave, without sufficient provocation by word or act, a misdemeanor; and subjects the offender, on conviction, to imprisonment not exceeding six months, and a fine not exceeding five hundred dollars.

"This act has received no judicial construction by the Court of Appeals. It has been several times presented to me on circuit, and I have given it construction. The terms 'shall *unlawfully* whip or beat any slave not under his charge, without reasonable provocation,' seem to me convertible. For, if the beating be excusable from reasonable provocation, it can not be unlawful. So, if the beating be either without provocation, or is so enormous that the provocation can be no excuse, then it is unlawful. What is sufficient provocation by word or deed, is a question for the jury. The question is whether, as slave-owners and reasonable men, if they had been in the place of the defendant, they would have inflicted the whipping or beating which the defendant did? If they answer this question in the affirmative, then the defendant must be acquitted—otherwise, convicted.

"The acts of 1821 and 1841 are eminently wise, just, and humane. They protect slaves, who dare not raise their own hands in defense against brutal violence. They teach men who are wholly irresponsible in property, to keep their hands off the property of other people. They have wiped away a shameful reproach upon us, that we were indifferent to the lives or persons of our slaves. They have had, too, a most happy effect on slaves themselves. They know *now*, that the shield of the law is over them; and, thus protected, they yield a more hearty obedience and effective service to their masters."

CHAPTER XIII.

OBJECTIONS THEORETICAL AND PRACTICAL.

IN resting slavery on contract, we remove the ground of those theoretical objections which impugn it as a system necessarily subversive of natural rights and upheld only by violence. Some of these objections have been sufficiently considered, but there is one which it may be well to subject to a fuller and more distinct examination.

The objection to which I refer, when simply enunciated, denies the right to buy and sell human beings. Sometimes the objection is rhetorically amplified, as when we are told that men have no right to traffic in human souls or make merchandise of human flesh ; and at other times it is stated with an appearance of philosophic precision, as when it is said that man can not rightfully hold property in man. But, however varied the expression, the exact point of the objection seems to be that no one human being can really own another, and consequently that men are not marketable commodities to be bought and sold.

The really remarkable thing in regard to this objection is, that the objector himself should believe that he has an antagonist. How comes he to think that when a man is said to buy or sell a slave he is understood to acquire or give an absolute right to the ownership of his person, body and soul? The idea is so extravagant, so contrary to all just conceptions of human nature, that one feels curious to learn something of its origin; and how it has come to pass that any man should entertain it himself or impute it to another. Who needs to be told that no man but himself can sell his own soul, and that only in a figurative sense, and with Satan for a purchaser? Who needs to be told that it is impossible for one man to make the body, limbs, and muscles of another his own? What man in this age and country will affirm that any man has a right to his own life, much less to the life of another? Few propositions, I think, can be more indisputable than that one man can not really own another, and consequently can not be said, in a *proper* sense, to buy or sell another. If I ask a bookseller the price of "Virgil" or "Juvenal," "Hume," or "Macaulay," does it ever enter his head that I wish to buy these worthies themselves, and become the owner of their muscles, as well as of the products of their minds? Was ever slave so stupid as to believe, when told to boil the kettle, that he must reduce the veritable iron to a fluid state and make it bubble with heat? How comes it, then, that when servants are said to be bought and sold, we do not see that the word *servants* is used by one of the most common figures of speech for the *service* which they owe? What else *can* be bought and sold among civilized and Christian people but the man's service or labor? When I read in the Scriptures, without a word of censure on the practice, that the patriarchs bought and sold slaves, and that the Levitical law enjoined on the Hebrews to buy servants of the heathen round about them and of the strangers that sojourned among them, and to make them their "possession," and to transmit them as an inheritance to their children after them "to inherit them for a possession;" it certainly never enters into my mind that the Hebrews thereby acquired an absolute right over the persons of their slaves, so as, if they pleased, to eat their bodies and destroy their souls; or, indeed, any other right to them than a right to their *service* and *labor*, and to the government of their persons in order to their service and labor. Nor do I suppose that any reader, left to the working of his own mind, would put any other construction on the language, or suppose that the heathen slaves are called the "possession" or property of the Hebrews in any other than a *limited* and *figurative* sense; the limitation so obvious that it needs not be expressed, the figure so natural that to avoid it would be a miserable affectation of philosophic precision. The servants were the possession or property of the Hebrews only for certain purposes, and even for these purposes they were not literally their possession, but merely called so by one of those common figures of speech, by which the cause is put for the effect, or the whole for a part.

All this seems to me to be so obvious that I doubt whether men in modern times would have put any other construction on the words were it not for the influence of a preconceived theory. They would read in the Old Testament that servants were a possession, and think (if they thought about the matter at all) that *servants* was put for *service* as naturally as when they read in the New Testament: "Lord, let me go first and bury my father," they think (if they chance to think of the matter at all) that only the *corpse* was to be buried; or, at all events, they would never dream of the "possession" involving an absolute right to the servant's body and soul, were not their minds prepossessed with certain notions of slavery that were as foreign to the Hebrew mind as they are, happily, to American practice.

Under the Roman law, in the palmy days of the Republic, there was nothing in the theory of slavery to restrain or limit the right of sale. Men were made slaves by captivity, and the slave was the property of his master to dispose of as he pleased. In the time of the Emperors the law restrained some of the abuses of the master's authority, but it never regarded the slave as under its protection. The theory was that the master had an *absolute* right to the life of the slave, a right which he held in abeyance on certain conditions, but which he resumed the moment that the slave refused his consent to those conditions; and, as the greater included the less, he had consequently the right to subject the slave to any treatment, however barbarous, which was short of death. On this theory the sale of a slave was the transfer of that absolute right to life and limb which the owner was supposed to possess. This theory of slavery, as we have shown, has been adopted by modern writers on civil liberty, and depicted in all its native horrors, in order to render the civil liberty which they have justly commended, more lovely and noble by contrast.

Slavery in the United States rests on a different foundation. The master has no right to the life of the slave, no *absolute* right to his person, no *absolute* right even to his service and labor. In no *proper* sense, therefore, can he be said to be the owner of the slave, and what he does not own himself he can not be said, in a *proper* sense, to give or transfer to another. He has a *conditional* right to the *service* of the slave; this *service* he may give or transfer to another, on the same *condition* on which he holds it himself; and the transfer of it for a valuable consideration is said, in legal and popular language, to be the sale of the slave. The law of the land, indeed, declares the slave to be his master's property, his "chattel personal," as the phrase is; and as the *service* is inseparable from the *servant*, I see not in what other way the law can secure the master's right. But to take such legal phrase in a philosophical sense, and to infer from it that the slave is neither a human person, nor a member of civil society, nor possessed of the rights (unless he had forfeited them by crime) of life and liberty (the liberty proper to his station), is to do injustice, I apprehend, both to the letter and spirit of the law.

The truth is, so far as I can see, that *the obligation to service for life*, on condition of protection and support, is the *essence* of American slavery. *Servitus in totum hominem non descendit*, says Seneca. The heathens saw, plainly enough, that slavery does not pass upon the soul; and we Christians know and proclaim by our laws that it does pass on the body, except so far as to secure from the slave that labor for life, the obligation to which is the essence of servitude.

The framers of our Federal Constitution touched the precise point of the relation, when, rejecting a word which has one meaning at Boston and another at Charleston, they referred to slaves as PERSONS BOUND TO SERVICE. The transfer of this right to service, or the sale of slaves, however common, is no essential or necessary part of the relation, but merely made a part of it by custom. The facility and frequency with which it is effected is, no doubt, one of the most revolting abuses of slavery, but it is one which may be greatly restrained, if not wholly removed, without impairing any essential feature of the institution.

"This continual change," says Judge O'Neall, in the

essay above referred to, "of the relation of master and slave, with the consequent rending of family ties among them, has induced me to think that, if by law they were annexed to the freeholds of their owners, and when sold for partition among distributers, tenants in common, joint tenants, and coparceners, they should be sold with the freehold, and not otherwise, it might be a wise and wholesome change of the law. Some provision, too, might be made, which would prevent, in a great degree, sales for debts. A debtor's lands and slaves, instead of being sold, might be sequestered, until, like *vivum vadium*, they would pay all his debts in execution by the annual profits. If this should be impossible, on account of the amount of the indebtedness, then either court, law, or equity, might be empowered to order the sale of the plantation and slaves, together or separately—the slaves to be sold in families."

It is certainly matter of the very deepest regret, that the reciprocal rights involved in the relation should be overshadowed in the public mind by the *master's right of property in the slave.* Perhaps this prominence of the legal question has been unavoidable; but, however this be, its effect has been most disastrous, by turning away public attention from the relation itself to one of its subordinate and most repulsive features.

Another objection, closely allied to the former, is, that slavery involves the breaking up of families, the separation of husband and wife, parents and children.

It is doubtless true, that the laws of the Southern States allow to the master a greater latitude in the transfer of his slaves than is consistent with the dictates either of humanity or of a sound and enlightened policy. Put yourself, then, in the place of your Southern brethren, and tell me frankly, Would you make the law of the State in all things the measure of your duty and the rule of your practice? Would you, in the spirit of greed and without mercy, grasp at every right which the law of the land concedes to you? Would not you govern your conduct by higher motives? Would not you act towards your dependents with that forbearance and clemency, with that kindness and charity which have their origin in a far higher source than legal prescriptions and statutes? What right have you, then, to charge upon your brethren a conduct which you would yourself despise? What right have you to think that they, in the transfer of their slaves, avail themselves, with reckless and avaricious temper, of the liberty which their laws concede? Or that they do not, in obedience to the dictates of humanity and religion, do all in their power to mitigate those rigors of slavery which the law of the land can not or does not reach?

But perhaps on this point you do justice to your Southern brethren; you admit that they do endeavor, and for the most part with success, to prevent the separation of families. But such, you argue, is their misfortune, such the withering curse of slavery, that they can not wholly remove this evil. Masters are sometimes cruel, creditors always merciless; and hence, from the inherent nature of slavery, these cruel separations will occur: southern planters can not prevent the evil, if they would.

Can *you* prevent it? Try the experiment first at home, and on freemen. Can you so adjust the mechanism of human society as to enable its members to earn their livelihood without the rupture of domestic ties? Can you prosecute commerce on this basis, or raise an army, or support a navy? Look round among your neighbors. Is there a family that has not been separated? and do you not find many whose members are scattered to the four quarters of the earth, driven to this separation by their wants, or by that sense of duty which is the sternest of all necessity? Have these separations caused no anxious thoughts, no sleepless nights, no bleeding hearts? Look at your jails and prisons, to which you send those incorrigible offenders who, in a different form of society, would be sold to some distant and rigid master; have the inmates of these dismal abodes left no relatives outside the walls that confine them to mourn over their disgrace, their incarceration and sufferings? What do we learn from this? That freedom has no advantage over slavery? God forbid! That slaves are not the lowest class of human society? We know that they are. But this we learn—that the evil under consideration is not peculiar to slavery; that it is incident to man in every age and country, every form and condition of society; that it falls equally, though in different ways and from the operation of different causes, both on bond and free; that if it produce greater sufferings among slaves than others (which I am apt to doubt) it has also, though we may not see it, a proportionate compensation; that we are bound to use our best efforts (in the way of duty and consistently with the order of human society) to avert this as well as other evils from those over whom it impends; and when these efforts have failed, then to acquiesce in the calamity as God's appointment; to receive it at His hands without peevish complaints and murmurs.

Another common objection to slavery is, that it proscribes marriage; slaves, it is said, being degraded by the necessity of their condition to the level of brutes, and compelled to live in a state of universal concubinage.

It was some time before I could discover the grounds of this objection. My inquiries of clergymen and others who had resided at the South satisfied me that marriage was recognized and respected by the bond in the church to which I belong, as well as by the free; that persons of both classes were married after the same form, and that no distinction was made in the performance of the rite, except that in the case of slaves the written consent of the master, or masters, to the marriage was required. My informants also assured me, that to the best of their knowledge, the same custom prevailed among other religious denominations. One clergyman, who has spent most of his professional life at the North, told me, that while residing at the South, he had himself solemnized more than fifty marriages among slaves; and he added, that the Roman Catholics (and I record the fact to their honor) make a point of the matter and insist on marriage among the slaves under their charge as a condition of cohabitation. With these facts before me, I was much at a loss to understand the grounds of this common statement in regard to the concubinage of slaves; a statement not confined to the slaves of remote plantations, but applied in the broadest terms to slaves of every description; and it is only since I have been engaged in the preparation of the present essay, that I have been enlightened on the subject. For this light I am indebted to a work entitled "The Higher Law in its Relations to Civil Government; with particular Reference to Slavery and the Fugitive Slave Law," written by WILLIAM HOSMER, published at Auburn, N. Y., 1852. In this work, page 90, as one of several illustrations of what he calls the "Natural Injustice" of Slavery, Mr. Hosmer gives us the following:

"5. *It* (slavery) *destroys the marriage relation.* So far as we have any knowledge, slaves are incapable of contracting marriage. They are, in this respect, exactly on a level with brutes. Indeed, it is not possible that marriage should exist, for marriage is a legal relation, and implies contracting power; but the slave can make no contract. He is unknown in law, except as belonging exclusively and entirely to another. He may live as if married, but it would be a desecration of law to repeat its forms over those who have not power to keep the slightest of its requirements. The slave, if he could be married, could not protect his wife from insult and defilement, for she would not belong to him, but to his owner—all that the slave has being his master's. Moreover, she might be sold or separated from him at any moment.

"6. *It destroys the parental relation.* This follows inevitably from the foregoing. When marriage is not allowed to exist, the duty of parents to instruct and provide for their children must cease. Amid universal concubinage, parentage can scarcely be traced beyond the mother," etc., etc.

From this passage it would seem that the astounding statements to which the public are treated on this subject, on both sides of the Atlantic, are gathered, not from an observation of facts, but from a process of argument. Marriage is a legal relation, and implies contracting power; slaves are by law incapable of contract, and consequently of marriage; therefore they live in a state of concubinage, and are degraded to the level of brutes!

Now, it is undoubtedly true that the State does not legalize the marriage of slaves; and for the same reason that it does not legalize the contracts of minors. Slaves are related to the State only through their masters, and it is not the province of the State, but of the master, to protect them, and to regulate their conduct. It is obvious, however, that contracts do not depend for their existence on the law of the State, for they exist before the law can recognize them, and give them validity. The slave who has a will and reason to understand the meaning of words has the essential qualifications for a contract, and is as capable of forming one as his master; and his contract, though destitute of *legal* force, will have the same *moral* force as his master's. He is, therefore, equally capable of marriage with his master; and his marriage, with his master's consent, though it have no *legal* validity, will be equally binding on his conscience. The difference is simply this: the marriage of the master is both a civil and religious contract; the marriage of the slave, with his master's consent, is a religious, but not a civil, contract. Is his marriage, therefore, null and void, because it has no *legal* force? When was it ever heard in the Christian Church, that marriage is only a civil contract? Is it not also, by the common consent of Christendom, a religious contract? Nay, is it not primarily and essentially a religious contract, prescribed by God himself? Have Christian States done more, or can they do more, than guard the contract, when made and ratified agreeably to Christ's institution, by annexing temporal advantages to its due observance, and temporal penalties to its infraction? What are we to think of men, claiming to be ministers of the gospel, who publicly declare that marriage, when solemnized according to Christ's institution, is not valid, merely because it is not legal? nay, is null and void, merely because the law of the State does not recognize and legitimate it? These men discover ANTICHRIST in the Church of Rome because, while she upholds the sanctity of marriage, she yet "forbids" it, from prudential reasons, to her priesthood; and yet, at the same time, without a suspicion of Antichrist in their own creed and practice, they proclaim it a "desecration" "to repeat its forms over" slaves, and thus discountenance, and virtually forbid, marriage among millions of their fellow-countrymen, under the impious pretense that it is not Christ but Cæsar, not the law of God but the law of the land, which can hallow their union, and restrain them from "universal concubinage"? "Thou hypocrite! First pull out the beam that is in thine own eye, and then shalt thou see clearly to take out the mote out of thy brother's eye!"

But the answer to this objection admits of illustrations which will possess an interest for many of the objectors, even if they fail to carry conviction. Time was, when the marriages of Quakers in Great Britain were void in law; were they then not valid and binding on the conscience, and were this estimable people justly liable to the charges which are now brought against slaves, because their marriages were not legalized? Take another case. The Independents, under Cromwell, took a fancy to dispense with the services of the ministers of religion, and contract marriages before justices of the peace. By the laws of Great Britain, which ignored the Commonwealth, those marriages were deemed illegal and void in law; and accordingly, after the Restoration, a statute was passed to legalize them. Did the Independents, after the Restoration, imagine that their marriages were not valid and binding on the conscience until they were legitimated by statute? Did the Church, or Parliament, while denying their legality, question their validity? I have read a good many high-flying sermons commemorative of "King Charles the Martyr," and denunciatory of the "Rebellion," but I do not remember ever to have seen this charge of concubinage brought against the Puritans, because their marriages during the "troublous times" wanted, as their opponents believed, the sanctions of the law of the realm, and, as they themselves vaunted, the solemnities of religion.

Whether the marriage contract would be better understood and observed among slaves if it could be legalized, is one of those speculative questions which it were useless to discuss. We are bound to take slaves as they are, namely, as persons standing in a mediate relation to society, and known to us only through their masters, by and through whom alone they are connected with society. In this respect they stand, as regards marriage, very nearly in the condition which minors held, until modern legislation made them capable of marriage without the consent of their parents; with what consistency or justice, while it still holds them incapable of other contracts which may prove infinitely less injurious to them than marriage, I stop not to inquire. The treatment of such cases is no new thing in the Christian Church. It was decided in her infancy; and the decision is attested by her ancient canons, and by the exposition which her Basils and Augustines have left of the grounds on which those canons were established. "If slaves," says St. Basil, as quoted by Bingham, "marry without the consent of their masters, or children without the consent of their parents, it is not matrimony, but fornication, till they ratify it by their consent;" for which he assigns this reason, "that contracts made without the consent of those under whose power they are, have no validity, but are null." With the consent of their masters, however, slaves are as competent to contract marriages, as free persons; and the marriages which they so contract are, when duly solemnized, as valid before God and His Church, and as binding on the conscience as they possibly can be; nor is it in the power of the civil state, by any law which it has enacted, or may hereafter enact, either to diminish or increase, by one iota, their validity, or the strength of their moral obligation.

If the ancient Romans, who had no higher conception of marriage than as being a civil contract, sought to excite the semblance of virtue in their heathen slaves, by calling their contubernity *figura et imago matrimonii*, we might surely expect better things of professed ministers of the Gospel, than to cast contempt on the marriage of Christian slaves, and to brand it as concubinage, for want of its civil sanction. Far more seemly would it be, as well as more consonant to God's ordinance, to cheer and encourage masters in the laudable efforts which many of them make to teach their slaves the nature and obligations of the conjugal and parental relations; to impress on masters also, kindly, but firmly, the awful responsibility and, possible guilt, of being instrumental in severing a union to which they have themselves consented; and to inculcate on the slave, as opportunity offers (and there can be no lawful opportunity without the master's permission), the duties which the Gospel of Christ enjoins both on the married and the unmarried.

There are other objections, some of which will come under review in a future chapter,* and others of which I do not feel called upon to consider. Indeed, I shall leave reason to be satisfied, if the interest which an author naturally feels in his subject has not already tempted me to transcend the object which I have proposed for myself; which is, not to recommend slavery, or to express a preference for the state of society which it involves, but merely to show that the form of slavery

* See chap. xvii.

which is protected by the laws in our Southern States, considered distinctly, in its essence, and as recognized by the Constitution of the United States, whatever be its incidental and concomitant evils, is not repugnant to the Divine law; and thus help to restore (if it please God to bless the effort), in some measure, the harmony which once bound together the North and the South; or at least to dissuade their sons from accustoming their hearts to war, and turning their mighty energies on the bowels of their common country!

> Ne pueri, ne tanta animis assuescite bella,
> Neu patriæ validas in viscera vertite vires!

CHAPTER XIV.

THE PERPETUITY OF SLAVERY.

There is, however, one objection which is thought to bear, with peculiar force, against the form of slavery that exists in our country, and which, from its collateral bearings, as well as its intrinsic importance, may properly form the theme of a separate chapter; and that is, that slavery in our Southern States is perpetuated from one generation to another. Slaves among the Hebrews, we are told, were capable of release on the Sabbatical year, and the year of Jubilee; and slaves among the Mohammedans have a similar privilege. Among the Greeks and Romans, slaves could be liberated from their servile condition, and when liberated could rise to such positions in society as their virtues merited, and lay the foundation of freedom and happiness for their descendants. But American slaves are cut off from all advantages of this sort; they are subjected to the evils of *caste*, from which they have no hope of escape for themselves, their children, or their latest posterity; they are doomed to slavery forever.

This, I confess, has always been, to my mind, one of the most painful features of slavery in our Southern States. In his struggle with poverty, and the troubles and sorrows that attend it, a man is naturally animated by the hope of some favorable turn in the wheel of fortune, which may lift him or his children, as it were, from the dust, and raise them to comfort and affluence. This hope is the light and solace of his soul, and the spring of its energies, and nothing can more effectually extinguish it than the certainty that both himself and his posterity are consigned to one hard lot forever.

But let us look at the matter calmly, and we shall see, I think, that this sad feature is neither peculiar to Southern slavery, nor consequent upon slavery at all.

It is not peculiar to our Southern States, but was found as well among God's own people, the ancient Israelites.

To reconcile this statement with the acknowledged fact of a periodical release from servitude, it should be noted that there were two kinds of slaves among the ancient Hebrews, the native, and the foreign, or Gentile slaves.

In the first place, the Israelites had slaves taken from among their own people. For, under the law of Moses, a man reduced to extreme poverty might sell himself, Lev. xxv. 39. A father might sell his children for slaves, Ex. xxi. 7. By an order of their courts, thieves, who were unable to restore what they had stolen, or the value of it, to the proper owner, might be sold in order to compensate the owner for his loss, Ex. xxii. 2, 3. And a creditor, also, might sell an insolvent debtor for the payment of his debt. There were other ways in which native Israelites could be reduced to servitude, but their bondage, however induced, was not perpetual; for, by a humane provision of the Mosaic law, these slaves had the option of liberty on every seventh or sabbatical year, and on every fiftieth year, or the year of jubilee, the liberation was peremptory and absolute, including those who had refused the liberty tendered to them on the Sabbatical year, and had voluntarily bound themselves to become slaves "forever."

The other kind of slaves, among the Hebrews, were those which they made from the surrounding nations. For they were permitted to buy the natives and subjects of these nations, and also such persons as had emigrated from these nations, and had settled in Judea. But the condition of these foreign, or Gentile slaves, was very different from that of the native, or Hebrew slaves. The latter were not to be ruled with rigor, and they were to be set free on the year of Jubilee; "For," saith God, "they be my servants, which I brought forth out of the land of Egypt." But slaves of the former kind had not this prerogative; for they might be treated with rigor. "Over them," says Calmet, "masters had an entire authority; they might sell them, exchange them, punish them, judge them, and even put them to death, without public process." Some of them were perfect proselytes to the Hebrew faith; others partially so, being called proselytes of the gate; both these might purchase their freedom, or be manumitted by their master, but neither the one nor the other had any claim to that periodical release which was the boon of the Hebrew slave. "The year of Jubilee," says Bishop Patrick (Lev. xxv. 45), "gave no servants of either sort their liberty."

Perpetuity of bondage, therefore, is not peculiar to the slavery in our Southern States, but finds its parallel in one form of that slavery which God permitted to exist among His ancient people.

But there is a further aggravation of our American slavery, to which it would be difficult to find a parallel. The Gentile slave owned by the Hebrew, if he bought his liberty, or was manumitted, and conformed entirely to the Mosaic religion, found himself, as respected his civil and religious rights and privileges, on a level with the Hebrews. The Greek or Roman slave, when enfranchised, was eligible to the honors of the State, and on a footing of social and political equality with its citizens; and the once despised slave, with no name of his own, might win for his master's name, which but for him would have been consigned to oblivion, present and future renown; as happened, we know, in the case of Terence. Not so with the American slave, who, though restored to liberty, is still his master's inferior, socially and politically. But is this the fault of slavery? Manifestly not. It is owing, in the first place, to the fact that the descendants of Africans in any of the United States, even when they become free, are not, and can not be, a portion of "the people" of the United States, in such sense as to be eligible to political honors, or even to the rights of citizenship. On this point, Chief Justice Taney is, I suppose, authority; and if he were not, the reasons which he gives for his opinion, and prescriptive usage under the Constitution, put the matter out of doubt. For, having stated the question, "Can a negro, whose ancestors were imported into this country, and sold as slaves, become a member of the political community, formed and brought into existence by the Constitution of the United States, and as such, be entitled to all the rights, and privileges, and immunities guarantied by that instrument to the citizen?" the Chief Justice remarks: "The words 'people of the United States,' and 'citizens,' are synonymous terms, and mean the same thing. They both describe the political body, who, according to our republican institutions, form the sovereignty, and who hold the power, and conduct the government, through their representatives. They are what are familiarly called 'the sovereign people,' and every citizen is one of this people, and a constituent member of this sovereignty. The question before us is, whether the class of persons described in the plea of abatement [the same as in the question above quoted] compose a portion of this people, and are constituent members of this sovereignty? We think they are not, and that they are not included, and were not intended to be included, under the word 'citizen,' in the Constitution, and can therefore claim none of the rights and privileges which that instrument provides for, and secures to, citizens of the United States. On the contrary, they were at that time considered as a subordinate and inferior class of beings, who had been subjugated by the dominant race, and, whether emancipated or not, yet remained subject to their authority, and had no rights or privileges, but such as those who held the power and the government might choose to grant them."

It is, therefore, no fault of Southern slavery, that its subjects, when emancipated, can not rise to political distinction, nor to social distinction, so far as it depends on political. The immediate bar to their social and political elevation, and which necessarily, though indirectly, operates to repress their hope of emancipation, and to keep them in slavery, is the fact, that the people who are held in slavery are not a portion of the people of the United States, or of the people for whom the government of the United States was intended. For this fact, slaveholders are not responsible.

But there is, moreover (as the Chief Justice intimates), another cause lying back of this; and that is the fact that, though of the same human *kind* with his master and his equal in all the essentials of that kind, in speech, reason, and will, the slave is yet of a different *race* from his master by characteristics which forbid the two to coalesce. You say, perhaps, that the refusal to amalgamate is unreasonable, and the consequence of cruel and shameful prejudices on the part of the whites. It may be so; on this point I would leave every man to his own opinion. Only I would have it observed that it is color and other physical differences between the two races that create the chasm that separates them; and that the sad feature of caste, which we all agree in deploring, is neither peculiar to Southern slavery, nor in fact chargeable upon slavery at all.

And, in view of the relation which the colored people of this country hold to the white, it does appear to me that a strong argument, on grounds of humanity and expediency, may be made in favor of a limited and regulated slavery, supposing such slavery to be, as I have endeavored to prove, permissible on the principles of universal justice and to involve no infraction of human rights. For, what are we to do with these people? I mean what are we to do *for* them with a view not to our own benefit but to theirs? In the Northern and Middle States we have abolished slavery, and I have no wish to deny that the measure was prompted in part by humane motives and the wish to benefit the colored population. But has it benefitted them? Are the colored people now more numerous, more loved, and respected than they would have been had no such measures been adopted? We risk nothing in affirming the contrary. We know that since they have been emancipated they have dwindled away; that they are debarred from social and political equality with their white brethren; that they are isolated and ostracized; and that in relieving them from *legal* slavery, we have reduced them to a *social* slavery, more cruel and capricious than that which was regulated by law. We have raised ourselves only to depress them. I should say that some of the Western States in excluding the colored population from their limits, had pursued, towards them, a course more intensely selfish, were it not that they have merely dealt out to them summarily and under the form of law the same treatment which we in the Northern and Eastern States have dealt out to them slowly and by force of opinion. I can not see that the Western States are much more to blame for their laws than are the Northern and Eastern States for their opinions. But the question recurs, and it is one in the answer to which we have all, North and South, East and West, a common interest. What are we to do with these people? Will you reënslave them in the Free States? This, even if you desired it, you can not do *justly* (as justice is distinguished from expediency), against their will; and with the opinions which they have imbibed from us, they account servitude a degradation to which they will never consent. Will you transport them to Africa? This again you have no right to do against their will; and if you consult them, they will tell you, almost to a man, that they love the country in which they were born, and prefer to stay at home. Will you remove the prejudices, if you please to call them so, of the whites, and induce them to raise their colored brethren to their own social and political level? Try first the force of your breath to blow back the torrent of Niagara! Every man who is not a very Quixote knows that such efforts, however laudable the motives that prompt them, are supremely visionary. If, then, the East can do no better for these colored people than doom them to social degradation, and if the West can give them no more than an inhospitable repulsion, why should either seek to disturb—why should not both unite to commend—the limited and regulated slavery under which they live and are happy at the South?

This state of fixed and clearly defined subordination, which precludes all jealousy and rivalry between the two races and enables them to work together for their mutual good, seems to be that which the providence of God designs. It is, if I may dare to say it, God's own determination of the great problem which the statesmen and philanthropists of our country have vainly endeavored to solve by their empirical schemes. I make no doubt that the Africans are the descendants of Ham and the Europeans of Japhet; and that both are, as descendants of Noah, partakers of the same humanity and concluded in the same redemption; while, at the same time, I think it undeniable that, wherever the two races are brought in contact, the peculiar physical and mental peculiarities of the one, whether brought about by the slow operation of natural causes, or by some supernatural interposition (like the confusion of tongues at Babel), the record of which has not been preserved, fit and dispose it to receive the care and protection of the other. It is not for man, indeed, to interpret the purposes of Divine Providence and to shape his conduct with a view to their fulfillment. It is a good distinction which the theologians make between the *Revealed Will* of God and the will of His *good pleasure*;* the former designed to train us to obedience, the latter to form us to habits of submission and adoration. I can not, therefore, agree with those who rest the right to hold Africans in bondage on the ground of the prophecy that Canaan should be the servant of Shem and Japhet, any more than those who rest the right of dominion on the superiority of the white race. The dictates of natural justice, the precepts of Revelation, are the rule of human conduct; if we follow this rule, we work with our Maker, if we deviate from it, we work against Him; and it is His prerogative to direct all human actions, whether just or unjust, whether peaceful or violent to the accomplishment of His own designs. But when He has been graciously pleased to unfold, in some measure, His design, in order that we

* Recte distinguunt Theologi voluntatem Dei, in voluntatem signi, et voluntatem beneplaciti; ac voluntatem signi appellant præcepta et prohibitiones, quibus Deus significat quid a nobis agi, vel non agi velit. Voluntatem beneplaciti nominant eam, quâ Deus vult absolute aliquid fieri, quæ semper impletur, et quam nulla vis externa impedire potest.—*Bellar. Contro. Chris.*, vol. iii., p. 987.

may see its fulfillment, and be the more convinced that the world and all its affairs are under His government; when we see that in fact He has overruled the violence of the wicked, and is using the willing coöperation of the righteous, for the fulfillment of His own prediction that Ham should be the servant of Japhet; we may assume, I think, *when justly devolved on us*, the charge and custody of the African, and exact from him that reasonable service with which he is justly bound to requite our care, in the humble, reverent, and grateful conviction—forced upon us by irresistible facts—that in so doing we are working together with God for the accomplishment of His wise purposes.

CHAPTER XV.

RENDITION OF FUGITIVE SLAVES.

THE Constitution of the United States provides, that persons held to service in one State, and escaping into another, shall not be liberated in virtue of any laws or regulations in the State to which they have fled, but shall be restored to the person from whose service they have escaped; and the Congress of the United States have enacted two laws declarative of this requirement of the Constitution, and designed to give it effect. These laws are commonly known as the Fugitive Slave Laws.

Now, the constitutional provision, as compared with the "higher law," or the law of Nature, must be either just or unjust. If just, the laws founded on it may be nevertheless unjust, through a failure to carry out its intent; but if unjust, the laws which declare and give effect to it must of necessity be unjust laws. Before we consider, therefore, the moral quality of these laws, it is obviously proper to examine the constitutional provision on which they are founded, and compare it with the law of Nature, in order to ascertain its justice or injustice, according to the standard of this law.

The dictates of natural law, by which I propose to test the constitutional provision, are those principles of *universal justice* which are assumed as the basis of the Justinian Code, and indeed of all legal and distributive justice. They are these *three: honeste vivere, alterum non lædere, suum cuique tribuere;* to live honestly, not to hurt any man, and to give every one that which is his due. If the constitutional provision is agreeable to these principles of eternal and immutable law, it is just; if contrary to them, it is unjust.

The words of the Constitution are: "No person held to service or labor in one State, under the laws thereof, escaping into another, shall, in consequence of any law or regulation therein, be discharged from such service or labor, but shall be delivered up on claim of the party to whom such service or labor may be due."

Now, it is not to be denied that a person may be held to service or labor unjustly. He may have done nothing, either expressly or by implication, to forfeit his natural liberty, have been seized by violence, and be held to service without color of law, and by the mere arbitrary and tyrannical will of the individuals who seized him. The man who kidnaps another, and holds him to labor by force and against his natural right, violates all three of the principles of universal justice; and had the Constitution sustained a claim which had no other foundation than lawless might, it had been flagrantly unjust. But the Constitution gives no countenance to acts of private and lawless violence. Its words are not, "No person held to service or labor," but, "No person held to service or labor in one State under THE LAWS thereof."

The case provided for, therefore, is that of a person held to service or labor UNDER THE LAWS of one State, and escaping into another; and the provision is that the fugitive shall not, in consequence of any law or regulation in the latter State, be discharged from such service or labor, but shall be delivered up on the claim of the party to which such service is due. Is this provision unjust in such sense as to contradict the principles of universal justice above defined? Undoubtedly it is, if the laws of the State, under which the fugitive is held to service, are themselves unjust. Does the Constitution, then, in providing for the satisfaction of claims to service in any one of the United States, assume that the laws under which the service is held are just and agreeable to the law of Nature, or unjust and contrary to this law? Or does it observe a profound silence and a strict neutrality on the question?

It is, indeed, an acknowledged and well understood principle, that each one of the United States is responsible for its own laws, and that the Constitution does not transfer this responsibility to the Federal Government, but leaves it as it found it, in the several States to which it properly belongs. And hence, it is argued in general, that the United States are in no degree responsible for the laws of the several States; and in particular that the laws under which persons are held to service in any one State, belong to that State exclusively, and in such sense, as that neither the Federal Government nor any other State is at all responsible for them.

But this principle, sound and highly important as it is in its legitimate application, can not, I think, be admitted without one limitation; a limitation which is assumed in the fundamental laws of every nation under heaven, and which the Preamble of the Constitution of the United States expresses in words: "We, the People of the United States, in order to form a more perfect union, establish justice, insure domestic tranquillity, provide for the common defense, promote the general welfare, and secure the blessings of liberty to ourselves and our posterity, do ordain and establish this Constitution for the United States of America." One end of the Constitution, therefore, is to ESTABLISH JUSTICE; not justice according to the laws of ancient Rome, or modern England; not justice according to any human code, but universal justice; or justice according to that eternal and immutable LAW OF NATURE, which requires us to live honestly, to hurt no man, and to render to every one his due. This universal justice, the breath and inspiration of the Almighty, when it lives in the habits and acts of a people, is the life and soul of which domestic tranquillity, the general welfare, and the blessings of liberty are but various forms and manifestations. And the very end and design of the Constitution is, not merely "to form a more perfect union," but to form a union and to establish justice; or to form a union which would be cemented by the bonds of universal justice; and the end proposed of necessity limits the means for its attainment, and must be kept in view in order to a just appreciation of those means.

When, therefore, the Constitution recognizes the laws of any one State, and provides that claims to service or labor under those laws shall not be reversed in any other State, it manifestly supposes that the laws so recognized and provided for are not repugnant to the dictates of universal justice. For the supposition is not to be endured that men designing to establish justice, insure domestic tranquillity, promote public good, and secure the blessings of liberty, should seek to accomplish this end by providing for the operation and guarding against the obstruction of laws or of rights and claims accruing under them, which are repugnant to natural justice, and consequently to the other above enumerated blessings which are inseparable from it.

It seems, therefore, necessary to believe that the case provided for in the Constitution is not that of persons held to service by arbitrary will, in opposition to law, nor of persons held to service under laws which are themselves contrary to universal justice; but it is the case of persons held to service under laws which are not contrary to universal justice. In effect, the case provided for is that of persons held to service JUSTLY; that is to say, in virtue of some relation which the law of Nature has established, or of some contract, express or implied, which the law of Nature binds them to fulfill.

Let us look, now, at the provision itself, which consists of two parts—the one negative, the other affirmative.

The negative part of the provision is, that the person held to service or labor in one State, under the laws thereof, and escaping into another, "shall not, in consequence of any law or regulation therein, be discharged from such service or labor."

In this clause, it is supposed that laws and regulations may exist in the State into which the fugitive has fled, which are in conflict with the laws of the State from which he has escaped; and it may be objected that if the laws under which a person is held to service in one State are just, then the laws which would work his discharge from service in another State must be unjust; and that consequently the Constitution, by recognizing the laws of both States, does not in truth concern itself with the justice of either, but merely aims to harmonize the operations of both, for the sole purpose of a union of the States, without regard to the justice or injustice of their respective laws.

The objection is specious; and I am the more desirous to fix attention on it, because the answer to it will put in a clearer light the point which I am endeavoring to establish.

I remark, then, that the objection rests on a confusion between *universal justice*, and *legal justice;* and vanishes the moment that this distinction is apprehended.

Actions which are enjoined on us by the law of Nature, or by those principles of this law which I have assumed as sufficient for the present inquiry, are intrinsically and universally just; and the rectitude which consists in an exact conformity to this law or to these principles, is called *universal* justice. On the other hand, actions which are defective in this kind of justice, or contrary to that law which requires it, are in *such sense* unjust as to be base and dishonest, immoral and impious.

Now, it is evident that between the rectitude which the law of Nature enjoins, and the wickedness which it forbids, are a great number of things which are neither commanded nor forbidden; and which for this reason are said to be *αδιαφορα*, or *indifferent.* And these indifferent things are the *proper* matter of human laws, because they are things in which the Divine law leaves us at liberty; which, if commanded or forbidden at all, are commanded or forbidden only by human laws; and which, when commanded or forbidden, we are directly obliged to do, or refrain from doing, in virtue of human laws. Every State or Commonwealth commands some things of this indifferent nature to be done, and forbids others, with a view only to present expediency, and on its own mere authority. And the justice that is agreeable to these human laws, which command or forbid things that are neither good nor evil, but are simply indifferent, and are commanded or forbidden by the State alone, and that not for their intrinsic rectitude or turpitude, but merely with a view to present expediency: I say, the justice which consists in conformity to these human laws, is that which is denominated *legal* justice.

These things premised, the answer to the objection is obvious. For the laws of the several States may be, and sometimes are, in conflict with one another in respect to matters of *legal* justice. Of these conflicts the Constitution is tolerant, and leaves them to be adjusted by the tribunals which it has created for the purpose. A position manifestly consistent with the point I am endeavoring to establish; which is, that the Constitution neither recognizes nor tolerates, but utterly abhors, all laws that are repugnant to *universal* justice; or, in other words, which decree things that are base and dishonest, or in any way contrary to the eternal and immutable law of Nature.

To apply the general proposition to the case under consideration. A person is held to service, for example, under the laws of South Carolina. Now what I affirm is, that the laws of South Carolina, under which this person is held to service, are not, in the eye of the Constitution, repugnant to the law of Nature or the principles of universal justice, because the Constitution itself is founded upon this law or upon these principles. The person so held to service in South Carolina, escaping into Massachusetts, might, we will suppose, unless the Constitution had interfered to prevent it, by the laws and regulations of this latter State, be discharged from such service. Why? Because the laws and regulations of Massachusetts contradict the laws of South Carolina in a matter of *universal* justice? No; but because they are at variance with them in a matter of *legal* justice; in other words, because Massachusetts, acting within the limits allowed by the law of Nature, has enacted sundry laws and regulations for the good of her Commonwealth, which laws and regulations South Carolina, keeping equally within the same limits, and availing herself of the same liberty which the law of Nature allows, has not seen fit to adopt, as not deeming them conducive to the welfare of her State. The Constitution tolerates both laws, because both are consistent with *universal* justice, and differ only in respect to matters of *legal* justice; or such matters as are undetermined by the law of Nature, and may be ruled, one way or the other, by every State, with a view to its own notions of the public good.

Let us turn now to the affirmative part of the proposition, which is, that said fugitives from service "shall be delivered up on claim of the party to whom such service or labor may be DUE." Due by what law? By the laws of the State, from which the person held to service has escaped? Certainly; this is the natural implication of the word, taken in connection with the rest of the sentence. Due by these laws only? Yes, if by the word *only* you mean to exclude the laws of the State or States into which the person held to service may have fled; but, No, if by the word *only* you mean to exclude the law of Nature or the principles of universal justice. Such a construction is abhorrent to reason, abhorrent to the spirit of the Constitution and to the circumstances under which it was created. For, suppose words to this effect had been inserted, and that instead of "To whom such service or labor may be due," the clause were to read thus: "To whom such service or labor, though not morally due, may be legally due, under the laws, namely, of the State to which the claimant belongs." Who can fail to see that such an avowal would have been an insult to the State in behalf of whose laws the provision was made, by imputing to them injustice, and also a virtual confession, on the part of the framers of the Constitution, that they themselves were willing to connive at injustice, to be accessories to it and copartners in it, in derogation of their own character, and in direct contradiction to their own solemn declaration, that they ordained the Constitution in order to "ESTABLISH JUSTICE." And if the clause can not bear the *expression* of such an intent, but repels it as an abomination, it is no less intolerant of the *implication*. Whence I argue that the service or labor, which is said in the affirmative clause of the provision to be "due" to the claimant, is assumed by the

Constitution to be due to him, not only under the laws of his own State, but also under the law of Nature; that is to say, in virtue of those principles of universal justice which bind men to live honestly, to do no wrong to others, to be faithful to their compacts, and to fulfill all their moral obligations.

I shall be told, probably, that there are other ways to get at the meaning of the Constitution, besides an examination of its language; that the opinions of the framers were adverse to slavery on *moral* grounds; that the Supreme Court has ruled slavery to be the creature of *local* law; and that these facts show that the provision of the Constitution for restoring to the claimant, outside of his own State, the service which is due to him under its laws, was made merely for the union of the States, and without regard to the essential justice or injustice of his claim.

Now, if this were indeed the case; if the framers of the Constitution made the provision under consideration merely with a view to the prosperity of the United States, and without regard to the principles of universal justice, how came they to be so fastidious in their language? Why so careful to eschew the words *slave* and *slavery*? If they had regard only to the public convenience, and not also to justice and moral rectitude, they might have provided, in plain words, for the recovery of slaves owned in one State, and escaping into another. Their studied avoidance of these words, and their guarded expression, *held to service under the laws*, are proofs, to my mind, that they had a sacred regard for justice, and were resolved not to promote the public good in opposition to its dictates.

But to come closer to the objection, I submit: 1. That the opinions of the framers, as gathered outside of the Constitution, are of no weight in determining its meaning, unless they meet the precise point for which they are adduced; and, 2. That even if they meet the precise point, they ought not to conclude, in opposition to the expressed design of the Constitution itself.

1. That the framers of the Constitution regarded slavery as morally wrong, if admitted, proves nothing to the purpose. For there are manifold forms of slavery, some confessedly unjust, and others indisputably just; and therefore the opinions referred to are not to the point, unless it can be shown that they were adverse to that particular form of slavery which consists in being *held to service under the laws* of one of the United States. That the framers of the Constitution condemned as unjust the slavery of ancient Rome, or of the West Indies, or even of the British Colonies before their independence, is no proof that they regarded, as unjust, a *service regulated by the laws* of any State that was embraced in the Federal Union.

2. But next let us suppose, for argument's sake, that the framers of the Constitution did hold this opinion; in other words, did regard as *morally unjust* that *legal*

servitude which was then existing, and which still exists in some of the United States; still I should say that we are not to be guided by this opinion in construing the provision under consideration, but that we are to gather the meaning of the provision from its own words, as compared with the declared intent of the Constitution itself. For as the result of the deliberative body can not be at all inferred from the opinions of some few of its members, seeing these may have been overruled by the rest; so neither can it be inferred with certainty, from the opinions of all expressed individually on other occasions, and in other ways. For the magnitude of the occasion, and the profound consciousness of the unspeakable responsibility devolved on them, may have raised them above themselves, above the age in which they lived, and restrained them from doing *collectively*, what they may have been willing to do *severally;* and the providence of Almighty God, watching over the foundations of a mighty empire, may have guarded them from the fatal consequences of their own errors, and guided them, by a Divine but sacred influence, to other decisions than those which were the mere fruit of human wisdom. It is the result by which we are bound, and not the process by which it was attained. Be it supposed, then (though I believe the supposition to be false), that the framers of the Constitution considered *legal* servitude, in all its forms, to be *morally unjust;* be it admitted, also, though I do not believe it to be true, that they were willing to connive at a gigantic injustice for the sake of profit or lucre, still the Constitution itself is paramount, and its distinct recognition of legal servitude in the several States in which it exists, its express provision for satisfying the claims of those who, under the laws of these States, had a right to the service or labor of others, when viewed in the light of its own avowed declaration, that it was ordained to ESTABLISH JUSTICE, oblige me to believe that this same legal servitude, the rights of which are thus scrupulously guarded, is, in the eye of the Constitution itself, morally right and just.

The further objection, namely, that judicial decisions, interpretative of the Constitution, represent slavery as existing in virtue of local and positive law, does not, as already intimated, touch the point for which I am contending. For I suppose, and have endeavored to prove in the previous chapters of this work, that the right to service or labor in the slaveholding States, is a right founded on the principles of universal justice, and one which the laws of those States are designed to declare and protect; just as the right to the service or labor of apprentices in the non-slaveholding States is a right founded on the principles of universal justice, and one which the laws of these States are designed to declare and protect. To meet the point, therefore, it must be shown, not only that the Constitution regards the right to service in the slaveholding States as upheld by local and positive law, but also that it regards this right to service as upheld by local and positive law *in opposition* to universal and natural law; and this is what the people understand, when they hear statesmen and judges proclaim that slavery is the creature of local and positive law.

Now, I am bold to affirm that the Supreme Court of the United States has never adjudged or declared that the right to service or labor under the Constitution is subject to this limitation. It could not do so, without proclaiming to the world that the right to the service of apprentices, and of all other persons bound to labor, is upheld in the United States by might and violence, in opposition to right and justice. The Supreme Court may not have declared that the right to service is founded in natural and universal justice; nor is it called upon to make this declaration, because its *proper* function is, not to expound and administer the law of Nature universally, but to dispense justice *under the Constitution and laws of the United States.* But, on the other hand, to declare that the right to service under the laws of any one of the United States, is contrary to universal justice, would be not only to transcend its proper functions as a minister of the Constitution, but it would be also to open the way for revolution and anarchy; because it would be an admission, or rather, a proclamation to the people of the United States, that the fundamental laws of their nation are repugnant to the laws of God and Nature. What the Supreme Court may do in future, the future only can reveal; but thus far it has been conservative, and not destructive of the government from which it *immediately* derives its powers; and has never even insinuated (would to God the same could be said of all the senators of the United States, as well as the judges of the Supreme Court!) the existence of a conflict, or of the least disagreement between the Constitution and laws which they are appointed and sworn to administer, and the "higher law" of Him "through whom kings reign, and princes decree justice."

So far has the Supreme Court been from evincing any such want of fealty to its sacred trust, that it has said all that it well could say within its appropriate sphere, to show that the right of service guarantied by the Constitution to the several States is a natural and universal right, a right created by the law of Nature; in the same sense as are all rights growing out of just and honest contracts, the fulfillment of which is a prime dictate of Nature. "The owner of the fugitive," says Chief-Justice Story, "has the same right to seize and take him in a State to which he has fled, that he had in the State from which he escaped; and this right to seize and recapture is universally acknowledged in the slaveholding States. It is no more than an affirmance of the principles of the Common Law applicable to the subject. The Court have no hesitation in holding that, under and in virtue of the Constitution, the owner of the slave is clothed with authority in every State of the Union to recapture his slave wherever he can do it without breach of the peace or illegal violence." * * * "The Constitution declares that the fugitive shall be delivered up 'on claim of the party to whom service or labor may be due.' A claim, in a just juridicial sense, is a demand of some matter as of right made by one person on another to do, or forbear to do some act or thing as a matter of duty."

Again: "The clause in the Constitution of the United States relating to fugitives, manifestly contemplates the existence of a positive unqualified right on the part of the owner of the slave, which no State law or regulation can in any way qualify, regulate, control, or restrain. Any State law, or regulation, which interrupts, limits, delays, or postpones the rights of the owner to the immediate command of his service, or labor, operates *pro tanto* a discharge of the slave therefrom. The question can never be how much he is discharged therefrom, but whether he is discharged from any by the natural or necessary operation of the State laws or regulations. The question is one, not of quantity or degree, but of withholding or controlling the incidents of a positive right." And once more: "The right to seize and retake fugitive slaves, and the duty to deliver them up, in whatever State of the Union they may be found, is under the Constitution recognized as an absolute, positive right and duty, pervading the whole Union with an equal and supreme force, uncontrolled and uncontrollable by State sovereignty or legislation. The right and duty are coextensive and uniform in remedy and operation throughout the whole Union. The owner has the same security, and the same remedial justice, and the same exemption from State regulations and control, through however many States he may pass, with the fugitive slaves in his possession, *in transitu* to his domicil." What more the Court could have said, without overstepping its proper bounds, to show that the right to service or labor, recognized by the Constitution, is *morally* as well as *legally* just, I am at a loss to conceive.

In the opinion that *local* law, when said to be the foundation of slavery, means the law of one place or country, as distinguished from other places or countries, and *not* as distinguished from the law of Nature, I am confirmed by the fact, that the same doctrine, viz., that slavery is the creature of local law, is held by the courts of those States in which slavery is regarded, not as a *foreign*, but as a *domestic* institution. Many cases have occurred in the courts of our Southern States, in which this doctrine has been avowed. In one, a case of more than usual interest, a suit was brought for the freedom of a mulatto girl, who had been bequeathed to a certain person, on condition that she should be freed on attaining her thirtieth year. The case turned on the construction of the will; and in the lower court it was decided against the slave, but on appeal to a higher court, the case was sent back for a new trial; not on the ground of an erroneous construction of the will, but on account of certain facts which had been incidentally proved. These facts were, that the slave had resided with the person to whom she was bequeathed for a number of years in France, by the laws of which country slavery can not be supported. The Court put their ruling upon the ground, that the relation of master and slave could only subsist by virtue of *local* law, and that as soon as slaves were voluntarily taken by their masters to a country whose laws did not support slavery, they were free; that there was always a presumption in favor of freedom; and that this was so strong, that the Court even went beyond the facts forming the essential part of the record. Now, is it to be supposed that the Southern Courts, in decisions like these, meant to convict the laws of their own States of injustice and hostility to the law of Nature? This were indeed a violent inference. The natural, if not necessary, inference is, that by *local* law, they meant the law of their own State, as distinguished from the law of other countries; and by presuming in favor of freedom, they meant to affirm the superior advantage and blessing of freedom, as compared with that limited and regulated slavery which their laws allow; both, however, being assumed to be consonant to Natural law or justice.

If, indeed, the Constitution mean less than this; if it guaranties to the Southern claimant the recovery of a debt of service which is only legally, and not morally, due, then, though I would not sanction the violent language of the abolitionists, yet I should be constrained to confess that the constitution has falsified its own profession of justice; and that George Washington, Hamilton, and Madison, Rufus King, Roger Sherman, and Benjamin Franklin, in their laudable effort to found a union of the States in justice, and to secure for themselves and their posterity the blessings of that liberty which is inseparable from justice, had signally and disastrously failed.

Assuming, however, what I have endeavored to prove, that slavery in our Southern States is founded in an implied contract; that, in virtue of this contract, the service or labor of the slave is a debt honestly due to the master; and that the Constitution provides for the recovery of this debt in States other than that to which the claimant belongs, I now proceed to consider the moral force of those laws which have been passed by Congress to give effect to this constitutional provision.

The Act of 1793 declares that, when a person held to labor or service in any of the United States, * * under the laws thereof, shall escape into any other of the said States, the person to whom such labor or service may be due, * * is hereby empowered to seize or arrest such fugitive, and take him before any judge of Circuit or District Court of the United States, residing or being in the State, * * * and on proof to satisfaction of such judge * * * that the person so seized doth, under the laws of the State from which he or she fled, owe service or labor to the person claiming him, it shall be the duty of such judge to give a certificate thereof to such claimant, which shall be sufficient warrant for removing the said fugitive from labor to the State from which he or she fled.

It further enacts that any person who shall knowingly or willingly obstruct or hinder such claimant in so seizing or arresting such fugitive from labor, or shall rescue him such fugitive from such claimant, * * shall for either of said offenses be subject to a fine of five hundred dollars.

The Act of 1850, which supersedes the former and is substantially the same, differing from it in several provisions designed to make the recovery more prompt and certain, fixes the penalty at one thousand dollars, and imprisonment not exceeding six months.

It appears, then, that these laws, carrying out the letter and spirit of the Constitution, assume that the service or labor of the fugitive is due to the lawful claimant, and that the fugitive has escaped in order to avoid the payment of a lawful debt; that they empower the claimant, in order to the recovery of the debt, to seize or arrest the fugitive; that they forbid all persons to hinder or obstruct the claimant in making the seizure or arrest, to rescue the fugitive after his arrest, or to harbor or conceal him knowing him to be a fugitive from labor; and that they subject to fine and imprisonment every person who shall be convicted of obstructing the claimant, in any of the above ways, in the recovery of his claim.

It is next to impossible for any law to be so framed as

to work exact and impartial justice in every case to which it may be applied. Be the laws ever so good, we shall sometimes need the rules of equity to remedy the defects and inconveniencies of legal justice. The laws under consideration are, from their very nature, peculiarly liable to this imperfection; and I doubt not that cases may arise under them, in which the fugitive is equitably entitled to that succor and sympathy which the law awards to the claimant. But the Constitution, I believe, and the laws founded on it, abhor injustice, and are conceived in the spirit of comprehensive benevolence; and before we consider the exceptional cases referred to, it may be well to look at the laws in their general bearing.

It must, I think, be admitted as a *general* rule, that the claimant has done nothing, and intends to do nothing to vitiate the virtual contract which gives him a just claim to the service or labor of the fugitive; that he has not treated him with merciless rigor or in any way abused his person, and that he does not intend to do so. This is evidently the supposition of the law which was not intended to work cruelty and abuse, but simply to compel the fugitive to render to his master the service or labor which he owes him; and we must surrender all faith in human nature unless we admit the supposition, as a *general* rule, to be reasonable and just.

Now, on this supposition it is to be observed that the law obliges us to no duty to which we were not obliged before its enactment. It is not the tyrant that the law sets before us, seeking to wreak his cruelty on the victim of his absolute power, but it is simply one man seeking to recover, in a lawful way, a debt of reasonable service from another. For the claimant, by the supposition, has fed and clothed his servant in infancy when the servant was unable to work, and the service which he claims is justly his due. We are, therefore, obliged by the principles of universal justice, to put no obstruction in the way of the claimant in any suitable and reasonable efforts which he may make to recover his debt; not to rescue the fugitive in case he is taken by the claimant, nor to harbor or conceal him. This is simple justice, and the law does but induce a *new obligation* on us to refrain from doing that which we were obliged to refrain from doing before its enactment. As a *general* rule, therefore, it seems clear that the requirements of natural justice, enhanced in their obligation by the laws of our country, forbid us to interfere between the lawful claimant and the person whose service he claims. In all ordinary cases, even if our sympathies are with the fugitive (who, for ought we know to the contrary, may be less deserving of them than the claimant), it does not appear that we can justly do more in his favor than see that the checks which the laws have interposed against an unjust claim be faithfully observed.

But suppose the fugitive, whether man or woman, to be flying from the claimant in fear of cruel treatment or abuse, and that the claimant aims to recover in order to inflict on him or her such cruel treatment or abuse. This I regard as an exceptional case; but on the supposition that it occurs, I admit that the fugitive has, on the principles of natural justice, the right to run away; and that, if we know or believe, on reasonable grounds, the facts that make it exceptional, we have the same natural right to further his escape. Nor does Divine Revelation, the best exponent of natural justice, contradict this opinion; for the precepts of the apostles and the canons of the Ancient Church, which command servants to obey their masters, and forbid them to decline their service, are *general* rules, and not framed with a view to such extreme and exceptional cases as may possibly arise.

But that we have the same liberty in view of the new and additional obligation induced on us by the laws of our country, is not so clear. For the law of the land has made specific provision against the injustice and cruelty which we apprehend; it has recognized the tribunals of the State to which the claimant belongs as vested with legitimate authority to restrain his power and to guard the rights of the fugitive; and though we may think this provision insufficient for the exigencies of the case, yet the law is paramount, and our judgment ought to yield to its direction. The case, indeed, must be extremely aggravated, and the proofs of its aggravation indubitably certain, before we should be justified, *in foro conscientiæ*, in deviating from the course which the law prescribes; and even then our justification would be found in the fact that we had neither defied the authority of the law nor rashly braved its penalties; but that, in the exercise of a sound discretion, we had acted in the spirit of the law, though in disregard of its letter, in a case for which it had failed to provide; and were, therefore, entitled, in reason and equity, to be regarded as exempt from its operation.

From what has been said, may easily be inferred the sentiments I entertain of the conduct of those persons at the North who encourage the slaves at the South to run away from their masters; who secretly harbor them, and furnish them with money to facilitate their escape, and who, from these and the like stealthy arts, are commonly known as "agents of the underground railroad." That these persons violate the law of the land, is, in my judgment, the least part of their guilt. I believe them to be not only *legally* but *morally* delinquent, instigators and abettors, directly, of fraud, and theft, and indirectly, and by consequence, of rapine and murder; fomenters of discontent and sedition; and I consider the credit accorded to them for philanthropy and manhood, to be the evidence of a perverted moral sentiment, and diseased state of the public mind. However, I am willing to look at the subject from their own point of view; and to inquire, inasmuch as they profess to be reasonable men and Christians, what conduct reason and religion demand of them in reference to the execution of the Fugitive Slave Law, on the supposition that their theory of slavery is correct.

Now, in the first place, it does seem to me that reason and common sense should teach them not to make for themselves a case which the law does not make. They have read, perhaps, in Rees' Cyclopedia, or in some other book of less repute, that a slave is "a person in the absolute power of a master with regard to his life, liberty, and fortune;"* or they have learned, perhaps, at third or fourth hand, from the worthy Dr. Paley, that "slavery is an obligation to labor for the benefit of the master, without the contract or consent of the servant;" and, under the influence of this foreign notion, they denounce the laws of their country, and seek to obstruct their execution, as if, forsooth, these laws were designed to uphold absolute power, and to wring labor from an oppressed and innocent people, without allowing them an equivalent in return! But this is a case of their own making; the laws of their country do not touch it in name or thing. They do not contain the words *slave* or *slavery*, and they do not relate to the thing which Rees and Paley, and other English authors, with their American imitators, express by these words.

* See the article "Slavery," in Rees, which appears to have been contributed by Clarkson, and is one of a hundred instances of the way in which the emissaries of new sects zealously avail themselves of the facility, or perhaps the venality of the editors of popular works to influence the public mind.

Dr. Paley's "slavery," as he himself explains, is limited to those who become "slaves," 1, from crime, 2, from captivity, and 3, from debt.

Slaves from debt are unknown in this country; and the others we do not call *slaves*, but *criminals* and *prisoners;* and their rendition, in case they escape from their appointed guardians, is provided for in other parts of the United States Constitution and laws than those now under consideration. And it is enough to move an honest man's indignation to see Dr. Wayland and others far less respectable than Dr. Wayland, apply Paley's definition to Southern laborers, who, as they know, are neither criminals, nor captives, nor prisoners; and then, taking advantage of their own deception, stir up the passions of the Northern people against the laws of the Union, as if they were designed to rivet the chains of the miserable, and not, as is the simple truth, to compel delinquent servants to pay an honest debt of labor.

Let men refuse to be duped any longer by the jugglery of words, and see for themselves the just and humane intent of the law; and if they do not mildly and firmly coöperate with it, they will at least abstain from officiously putting obstacles in the way of its legitimate execution.

But to come nearer to the point. These men, we will suppose, honestly believe that the claimant has only a *legal*, and no *moral*, right to the service of the fugitive; that the fugitive has never, by any act of his own, express or implied, parted with his natural right to the use of his liberty, but still retains this right; and that the law which commands the fugitive to be restored to the claimant is *unjust*, as compared with the principles of universal justice or the law of Nature. This, our opponents may say, whether it be right or wrong, is our honest conviction; and, as you promised to look at the matter from our point of view, we should like to know what course, in reference to this law, you think that we, as reasonable men and Christians, are bound to pursue?

To these persons I answer that, if the law required them to assist, or be in any wise actively instrumental, in the recovery and restoration of the fugitive, they would not, in my opinion, with their present views of the subject, be bound to comply with it in these particulars and to this extent. In a case like this they are not, in my opinion, obliged by their Christian profession to render an *active* obedience to the laws of their country; but they are to refuse, firmly and respectfully, to have any agency in carrying them out, submitting themselves, at the same time, cheerfully and patiently to their penalties. This is the course which the Apostles themselves, and all good Christians after their example, have pursued when the law of the land has commanded that which the law of God has forbidden; they have resolutely obeyed the Divine law, and endured the penalty of the human. Nor is this merely the command of Revelation, but the dictate also of Nature and right reason; as we learn from the heathen Socrates, who refused to accede to the entreaties of his friends, that he would escape out of prison, and resolutely preferred to suffer the death which his judges had decreed.

This view of the case applies, indeed, to those who hold office under the Federal Government, and who are required by their official duty to side with the claimant, and assist him in the recovery of the fugitive. Such persons, if they can not with a good conscience enforce the law, and deliver up the fugitive to the claimant, are obliged, I think, to refuse to do so; and either to abide the consequences of their refusal, or avoid them by the resignation of their office. But the law under consideration gives no private citizen the opportunity to become a martyr if he would. For it requires of him no *active* obedience whatever for the recovery of the fugitive;* its requirements for this purpose are negative; it requires him to put *no* obstruction in the way of the claimant, *not* to harbor or conceal the fugitive, but simply to let both parties alone. I confess myself utterly at a loss to conceive on what grounds of reason or religion any man, who acknowledges himself bound to obey the laws of his country, in all cases in which they do not contradict the law of God, should refuse to obey his

* True, in case attempts are made to thwart the law, its agents may call in the aid of the *posse comitatus;* not, however, to recover the fugitive, but to restrain those who factiously aim to defeat the law.

country, when she merely commands him to do *nothing;* when she requires him only not to interfere between two disputants, and asserts her own right to settle the dispute in her own way.

On the whole, then, it seems to me that, as reason and common sense should teach men not to conjure up to their fancy a grievance which the law does not impose; so reason and religion should teach those who are *conscientiously* opposed to this law to remember, that their country has a conscience as well as they; and that, however they may think themselves right, and their country wrong, yet since she requires them to do nothing contrary to *their* conscience, they should at least forbear to do anything contrary to *her* conscience.

CHAPTER XVI.

THE AFRICAN SLAVE-TRADE.

THAT was a sage piece of advice which Phaëton gave to the youthful Icarus when, having adjusted to his body his wings cemented with wax, he essayed to fly over the Ægean Sea—*Medio tutissimus ibis.* The middle course is your safest. If you soar too high, the sun will melt the wax, and, losing your wings, you will fall headlong into the sea; if you keep too near the earth, the cold will stiffen the wax, and, unable to use your wings, you will be tossed about, the sport of the winds. If you would fly with safety, use your wings in the element that Nature provided for them, and take care neither to rise above nor to sink below it.

To apply the vailed wisdom of the fable to the subject before us. They who own no law but force, who proclaim with the ancient Athenians their purpose to invade and enslave any people that in their opinion are *fit* to be made slaves, who, in scorn of justice, take advantage of the weakness of their fellow-men to use them for their own base and selfish ends, sink beneath the just level of humanity, deprive themselves of the light and warmth which Revelation and right reason afford, and are tossed about in the cold regions of selfishness, the sport of avarice and of their other turbulent appetites and passions. They, on the other hand, who soar on high, after the fashion of the French philosophers and the German transcendentalists, and attempt to adjust society on their airy abstractions of liberty and equality, are predestined to a miserable failure: no sooner do they reach their pure ether of bliss than suddenly the wax melts, and they fall headlong to the earth. Witness Fourier and Owen; witness also the Genius of Albion, poising herself on high on the waxen wings of French freedom and Scotch philanthropy—over the island of Jamaica!

The middle course is the safest; but by a middle course let me not be understood to mean a compromise, or an expedient in which truth and error are mutually conceded and accepted, in order to oppose a temporary stay to evils, which can only be permanently abated by removing their cause. No; if with the Roman poet I condemn extremes, it is for the reason which he assigns; viz., that Truth and Rectitude are only to be found between them, and can not exist in either direction beyond them.* For I can not agree with those who represent madness and mischief as the excesses of truth and justice, or who, to speak in the concrete, would have us believe that the insane schemes of the abolitionists are

* Est modus in rebus, sunt certi denique fines
Quos ultraque citraque NEQUIT CONSISTERE RECTUM.

the result of sound premises rigorously carried out to their logical consequences. I would have men persistently and fearlessly follow truth whithersoever it may lead them; and when they counsel madness and mischief, I am more apt to suspect the fallacy of their premises than of the argument that is raised on them. Moderation is the path of wisdom, and though men may be moderate from indolence or habit and without the ability to develop logically the grounds of their action or inaction, yet they can not be extravagant without folly. All truth lies between opposite errors, all virtue between opposite vices; but is that a reason why men can not be truthful and virtuous, aye and follow out every principle of truth and virtue to its farthest legitimate consequences, without becoming contaminated with error and vice? Religion, the doctrine of right reason and revelation, lies midway between superstition and atheism; can not a man, then, be religious, so as to think and do all that Reason and Revelation demand, without being either superstitious or an atheist? Temperance lies midway between gluttony and asceticism; can not a man be temperate without being either a glutton or an ascetic? Prudence in our affairs is a mean between prodigality and covetousness; does prudence then really consist in a mixture of these vices, and is it not rather an avoidance of both? And so with all truth and all virtue; nor should I have any fault to find with any class of fanatics for carrying out their "one idea" to its legitimate consequences, provided their "one idea" were founded on truth and justice. For by no possible application of right reason can any principle of truth and justice be made to exceed the limits of truth and justice.

But men are governed more by passion than by reason; and hence it happens in morals, as in physics, that one extreme leads to another. Excessive heat prepares the atmosphere for a storm; and when the storm has exhausted its fury, it is succeeded by a calm proportioned to its violence. Superstition begets Atheism, and Atheism in its turn drives us back to superstition. And the passions which impel some beyond the limits of right reason in one direction, disgust others, and impel them beyond the same limits in the opposite direction. Hence the licentiousness and free-thinking of one age, are a reaction from the sanctimony and hypocrisy of the age preceding; the intemperance of one generation drives the next into a sort of savage austerity; and hence, to bring this tedious proem to a close, men recoil from the horrors of the African slave-trade to the ruthless abolition which proscribes all servitude; and again, disgusted with the folly and insane violence of abolition, they learn to revert with complacency and a stupefied conscience to the meanest and most atrocious form of human iniquity.

The best way to arrest the passionate excitement which impels men to opposite extremes, is to define distinctly, and to impress on their minds, that middle course of truth and rectitude which reason prescribes. For, to obliterate the lines which separate any virtue from the vices that bound it on either side, is, in effect, to blot that virtue out of existence, and to leave the opposite vices to struggle for alternate dominion.

And the middle course, the course of rectitude and safety, on the subject under consideration, is one, happily, which we are not to seek. It is made to our hands; not proposed for our consideration and future adoption under the sanction of great names, but already clearly defined, and bound upon us by the highest human and divine authority. For, to guard effectually against the seditious schemes of abolition on the one side, and the reopening of the African slave-trade on the other, we have only to adhere faithfully and resolutely to THE CONSTITUTION AND LAWS OF OUR COUNTRY. And the Constitution, as far as relates to the present subject, is no compromise. From whatever extreme opinions they who framed it may or may not have receded, there is no mixture of truth and error in the result at which they arrived. There, at least, they have spoken with no "stammering lips," no strange tongue. The provision of the Constitution, in regard to servitude, compromits no principle of truth, and contains no ingredient of error. It is a pure and unequivocal enunciation of justice and wisdom. It meets the fact, the existing, undeniable fact, that a numerous class of persons in our country are bound to service; and it provides, in certain emergencies, for coercing them into a fulfillment of their obligations for delivering them up, in case they escape from one State into another, to the parties to whom the service may be due. On the other hand, it gives no sanction to lawless violence, and justifies no infraction of human rights; but prepares the way for the National Legislature to denounce and forbid, as it has in fact denounced and forbidden, the seizure and enslavement of men in foreign lands, and their importation into our country. Thus the Constitution has done for us, what, in our present state of excitement and bewilderment, we could not do for ourselves; it has marked out for us the course of safety and rectitude, and has guarded us from injustice and lawless violence on the right hand and on the left. And the Constitution, and the laws founded on it, are the rule of the national conscience; a rule so consonant to right reason and Revelation, that they who deviate from it, either to the right hand or to the left, are recreant, not only to their country, but to the law of Nature and to the law of Christ.

If the Constitution and laws of the United States regard the limited and lawful slavery that exists in our Southern States as a stupendous sin, upheld by absolute power against right, and tolerated only from necessity, it would be impossible to vindicate their consistency in protecting slavery and denouncing the slave-trade, without denying to them that which is worth much more than consistency, the profound reverence which they profess to entertain for JUSTICE, LIBERTY, and THE RIGHTS OF MAN. For slavery, on this theory of it, is as really, though not so flagrantly, opposed to justice, liberty, and human rights, as the slave-trade; and, on the other hand, it is quite probable that that fancied regard for the public good which statesmen are apt to mistake for necessity, as it has been invoked both in Great Britain and in this country, may at any time be invoked again in justification of the slave-trade, as well as of domestic slavery. If the Constitution and the laws of the United States protecting slavery in those States in which it has been established, and at the same time prohibiting the slave-trade, have no deeper foundation than a baseless and temporising expediency, then they can not be sustained among a free and high-minded people who have a paramount regard for truth, honor, and justice: they will perish, as they deserve to perish, loathed of all good men, and disowned of God. For if slavery, as domesticated among us, be regarded as a sin tolerated and protected by the Constitution merely for the sake of the material advantages that flow from it, what adequate security has the South that this protection will not be withdrawn? And, on the other hand, if the slave-trade be regarded as an evil of the same kind, and be interdicted for no higher reasons, what security has the North that the laws interdicting it will not be repealed, and that they themselves will not join in their repeal, if, by some turn of affairs, it should seem to be for their interest to repeal them? For it is a law of nature that action and reaction are equal; and when the furious blast of the abolition agitation shall have spent its force, it will be but natural that it should be followed first by the secret agitation, and next by the open advocacy of the slave-trade. In this view of the subject, the Constitution and laws of our common country are baseless and mutable, having no ground of permanence, no claim to reverence. Or rather, we *have* no fundamental laws, but are, as we are sometimes reproached with being, a nation void of principle, and ready to legislate in any direction from cupidity and the lust of dominion. But if the Constitution and laws of our country are really founded, as I believe them to be, on the enduring principles of justice, liberty, and human rights; if they protect the limited slavery that is already established among us because it is consistent with these principles; and if they denounce the African slave-trade because it is a gross and wanton infraction of these principles, then indeed we may have faith in their permanence; for then the Constitution and laws of our Union are settled on foundations more durable than the everlasting hills; and all who live under them, North and South, East and West, may, as men, citizens, and Christians, unite as one man in their triumphant vindication and support.

In all that I have advanced in defense of slavery, as it is established under the laws of our Southern States, I have regarded the slaves as men, made in the image of their Maker; and I have insisted on man's natural right to the use of his liberty, and on the injustice of depriving him of it by violence, and without some act or acts of his own that involve a surrender of it. From this theory of slavery, it is manifestly impossible to draw any valid argument in favor of the violent seizure or purchase of native Africans with a view to their transportation, sale, and enslavement in other countries. The two things are utterly unlike; the one being, as I have endeavored to to show, a fulfillment of the laws of Nature, and the other being, as is plainly manifest, an unmitigated violation of these laws. And it is because of their utter dissimilarity, that the Constitution and laws of our Union have extended the shield of protection over the one, and fixed the ban of reprobation on the other: and for the same reason, our Southern brethren, while approving and upholding their own social institutions, are as free, in point of consistency, as are we at the North, to condemn the African slave-trade; and as much bound to do so by a consistent regard to the sacred rights of humanity and justice.

The wisdom and justice of the Constitution are as manifest, in my opinion, in regard to the slave-trade, as in regard to the slavery which it found already established. It discriminates the two by the broadest line of demarcation With the origin of slavery in the several States that had legalized it, it did not meddle; but, accepting slavery as a fact, in the providence of God, already established, and acknowledging the sacred obligations of mutual protection and service which it involved, it wisely and justly provided for the fulfillment of those obligations. But the seizure, purchase, and importation of free persons from abroad, to be reduced to slavery within the limits of its jurisdiction, was a very different matter. This was confessedly an evil, a wrong, a violation of justice. The Constitution, consistently with its design, could not approve this injustice; nor, in fact, does it say one word which can, by any possibility, be tortured into an approval. It recognized the slave-trade as an existing evil, but as an evil which it was not in the power of human government immediately to abolish. Justice demanded its extirpation, and wisdom counseled that, like all deeply-rooted evils, which are only aggravated by the application of rash and ineffectual remedies, the extirpation should be gradual, in order to be certain; and hence, with united wisdom and justice, the Constitution makes the following provision: "The migration or importation of such persons as any of the States now existing shall think proper to admit, ill not be prohibited by the Congress prior to the year e thousand eight hundred and eight; but a tax or duty ay be imposed on such importation, not exceeding ten dollars for each person." The permission to import slaves under the laws of any State, up to a certain time, is an implied, indeed, but an imperative prohibition, of such importation after that time; and on this prohibition, contained in the Constitution, Congress has grounded its stringent laws in respect to the slave-trade.

Thus the Constitution and the laws declarative of it, are like a two-edged sword, which deals death to injustice and impiety on the right hand and on the left. Servitude, and the rights involved in it, when it has passed beyond human control, and become, in the providence of God, interwoven with the fabric of human society, are protected from the invasion of ruthless fanatics, and the intermeddling of pragmatical busy-bodies; while the slave-trade, which involves no social ties, which has not a shadow of foundation in justice, which is, in its inception, its career and its consummation, pure and unmitigated villainy, is proscribed, that it may be, as far as possible, abolished and eradicated from the face of the earth.

But let us look more particularly at the laws respecting the slave-trade, and the reasons for them.

The native inhabitants of Africa are in a wild and uncultivated state; uncivilized, unchristianized. The thought of waging a solemn war against any of these ignorant tribes is preposterous. The nations of Europe and the United States may sometimes find it necessary to resort to severe measures, in order to compel their observance of contracts, or to restrain them from wreaking their savage cruelty on the colonists and emigrants who have settled on their coasts: but in this warfare, if such it may be called, it is no part of the policy of civilized nations to make or retain prisoners, much less to reduce prisoners to a state of servitude. Their object is to protect the colonists, or to punish perfidious tribes. In the prosecution of this object, it may occasionally be necessary to capture prisoners for some temporary purpose, possibly to put them to death, in order to strike terror into the native tribes. Such cases, however, are comparatively rare. The capture of prisoners, under national authority, is not the way, in fact, in which African slavery has been originated and introduced into Christian countries; nor is it to be supposed that any enlightened nation of the present age would capture prisoners for the purpose of making them slaves, much less proclaim a foreign people, however weak and ignorant, enemies, for the sake of making them slaves. Such a course would be in violation of the law of Nations; that is to say, of those principles of the law of Nature by which Christian and civilized nations have consented to be governed.

If the seizure of native Africans for slaves is to be effected at all, it must be effected hereafter, as it has been heretofore, by individuals, or associations of individuals, acting on their own responsibility, independently of the nation or nations to which they belong, and, in most cases, in violation of their laws.

By what possible motives can such seizure be justified? The Africans, in their own country, however untutored and barbarous, have that right to freedom which belongs, by nature, to all mankind. On what ground of justice can an invader, whatever pretensions he may make to Christianity and civilization, or whatever desires he may affect to have for the diffusion of these blessings, deprive them of this right by violence? In vain will he allege, in his justification, that the descendants of Africans are held in slavery in Christian countries, and under Christian laws. This fact is in no respect a precedent, and furnishes no shadow of excuse for his seizure and transportation of free and native Africans. For, have they or their parents lived on his bounty? Has he fed, and clothed, and sheltered them, and reared them to man's estate? Is he bound to guard their natural rights to life and liberty, to maintain them in sickness and decrepitude, and to provide for their offspring? Does he stand in any relation to them on which he can found a just claim to their service? If not, on what fact can he rest to justify himself in seizing them and treating them as slaves? Or, having seized and appropriated them, on what fact can he rest to justify himself in regarding them as his property, and selling them to others? Certainly none; the relation in which these free natives stand to him, and the relation of lawful servants to their master, are as far asunder as the poles; they owe him no labor or service, no gratitude, no affection, no debt of any kind. His seizure of them is an act of sheer diabolical violence, without the faintest shadow or semblance of justice to mitigate its atrocity.

It is an act all through and all over abominable, and forever to be detested of God and man.

An act of singular and acknowledged impiety and infamy, but without an appropriate name. For by what name shall we designate it? It is not precisely theft, or robbery, or kidnapping, or any other crime; for these acts, and indeed all crimes, in the technical sense, are offenses against municipal law. But these Africans are under the jurisdiction of no civilized or Christian people; he who seizes them, therefore, breaks none of those laws by which his own nation protects its citizens and inhabitants in the enjoyment of their rights and liberties. Nay, he is himself an outlaw, and rests his bodily safety on the fact that he is out of the reach of the laws of his own and of all civilized nations. He makes himself AN ENEMY OF THE HUMAN KIND, and sets at open defiance that law which is the basis of all municipal law, the law of Nature itself. In these respects he resembles the PIRATE, and differs from him only in making the the land, instead of the water, the scene of his depredation. Hence, although his offenses are not really piracy, yet they are justly declared and accounted piracy, by the laws of Christian and civilized nations; and he himself, and all who are accessory to his offense before it is committed, are justly treated as pirates, and exposed to the scorn and hatred, not of one nation only, but of all mankind.

But some, perhaps, disclaiming and denouncing the

wanton seizure of Africans on their native soil, may yet assert the right, and even make a virtue of buying them, in order to save them from death. It is possible, indeed, that a case may happen in which the negro, to escape from torture and death, may consent to go into servitude, under promise of protection and humane treatment. But such cases, if not wholly imaginary, are at least so rare as not to be worth taking into account. The purchases effected by the slave-trader, and by which alone his traffic can be made to gratify his cupidity, are of a widely different kind. He sets up a market for negroes, and buys them of any one that will decoy them to the coast, and deliver them into his possession. Instead of seizing them himself, he stimulates others to seize them, and, for rum, or money, or a few paltry trinkets, he avails himself of the rapacity and violence of his agents. Or he whets the avarice and cruelty of one tribe to make a prey of others, and buys captives of the conqueror; thus instigating the native tribes to mutual and fiendish wars, for the mere purpose of making prisoners, and selling them to the traders.

The plea that the captured are prisoners of war, and sold and bought according to the right of war, is one of those infamous pretexts with which hypocrisy seeks to varnish deeds of villainy with a show of decency. In no just war, much less in an unjust, has the captor a right to the life of the captive. The law of Nature gives no man a right over his own life, much less over the life of another man; it permits us, indeed, to take the life of an enemy when the doing so becomes necessary to defeat injustice and violence; but when an enemy becomes a prisoner, this necessity ceases to exist; and to deprive him of his life without necessity is murder. The sale of a prisoner, therefore, founded on this pretended right of war, is essentially unjust; not only null and void, but vile and abominable, as being an offense not necessarily against municipal law, but necessarily and always against that law of Nature which all mankind are bound to observe and to vindicate. The man, therefore, who buys a negro on this pretext, is a partner in guilt with him who seizes and sells him. Less bold, perhaps, but more base and sneaking than the kidnapper, he is deservedly placed in the same category with him, and branded as an enemy of the human kind; and if he does not know the atrocity of his nefarious traffic, it is well that the municipal law should teach it to him, by declaring, as the laws of the United States do declare, the purchase of negroes unlawfully seized to be equally PIRACY with the seizure itself.

To evade the force of these arguments it is sometimes contended that the African negroes belong to an inferior race, and that the white, or superior race, has, on the ground of its superiority, the right to seize and transport them into distant countries, and reduce them into slavery.

I am not sure that I understand this argument. Divine Revelation, in this, as in other matters, giving distinct utterance to the voice of Nature, informs us that God, having created man, blessed him, and gave him DOMINION over the beasts of the fields, over the fishes of the sea, over the fowls of the air, and over every living thing that moveth upon the earth. It is on this grant of our Maker, inferred by reason, expressed by Revelation, that we rest the right of man to dominion over the brute creation. The subject of the grant is man, mankind, all men; and the matter of the grant is an absolute and universal dominion over all other creatures on earth. Man can not be at once the subject and the object of the grant; no man, therefore, has an absolute right to use other men, but every man and all men have the right to use inferior creatures for their benefit.

They, therefore, who would justify the seizure and enslavement of African negroes on the ground of their inferiority, are bound to explain their meaning. Do they mean that the blacks are inferior to the whites in kind? that the whites constitute the entire human kind, and that the blacks are not included in this kind? If this be their meaning, then, the consequence is good. For man is lord of the earth, and has a just title to dominion over creatures inferior to himself in kind; and by the same right that he subjugates other inferior creatures to his use, some for food, others for clothing, others for labor, he may seize the negro and doom him to servitude, or make any other use of him he sees to be for his own advantage. But, though the consequence be good, the premise is utterly false. For, let men magnify the differences as they will, between the two races, they are, after all, accidental, and not essential. The color of the skin, the quality of the hair, and the peculiar anatomical structure which is supposed to give acuteness to the senses of the negro at the expense of his intellectual vigor, do not enter into the definition of man. The erect figure, the power of articulate speech, the reasonable soul, with its marvelous endowments of conscience and will, are attributes of the black as well as the white; and these constitute the man. If they mean that the inferiority is not in kind, but in degree, then, though the premise is good, the consequence fails; for both being of the same kind, have the same natural rights to life and liberty; and the superiority of bodily or mental conformation gives the one race no more right to lord it over the other, than one man's strong habit of mind or body gives him a right of dominion over his feeble neighbor.

Again, it is argued by some who admit the iniquity of the slave-trade, that it is impossible to repress it; that its cruelties are greatly increased by its secret and contraband character; and that, therefore, a humane policy demands that government should permit it.

There are three ways in which an evil may be permitted by the municipal law.* The law may wholly

* See Bp. Sanderson's Sixth Prelection, De Leg. Human. Materia, Sect. 18.

pretermit and pass it by, and in this way it must permit many evils, it being the singular prerogative of the Divine law to prohibit all evil. But the slave-trade is too public and audacious to be passed by in silence; a permission of this sort would, under the circumstances, be tantamount to an approval. Again, the State may define certain limits, beyond which an evil shall be guilty and punishable, and within which it shall be innocent and safe. But this sort of permission can only be extended to evils which are not essentially such; by which I mean such as are not forbidden by the Divine law, either natural or positive, but are entirely within the power of the State, and are the proper matter of human laws. But piracy, or evils equivalent to it, are not of this sort; the State can not make them innocent in any form or degree, nor extend protection to their perpetrators and abettors. Again, an evil, essentially such, may be so deeply rooted that it is impossible to eradicate it by prohibitions; and then the State, with a view to regulate an evil which it can not abolish, may tolerate it by imposing a tax or fine, and making it a source of revenue. This is a desperate and perilous sort of legislation, one which is common under the worst governments of the old country, but which has never, to my knowledge, been adopted in this country, either by our State or Federal Governments, unless the action of the Federal Government, in respect to the slave-trade, be an exception. For Congress did, in the beginning of our national existence, in this way permit the slave-trade for a limited time, laying a tax on every slave imported. It *may*, I suppose, without transcending its function as a minister of the law of Nature, do the same thing again, if demanded by a manifest expediency. But as the effect of the prohibition of the slave-trade has been to guard the slavery established among us before our independence, from accessions by violence, and thus to allow its growth and expansion as a just, peaceful, and orderly institution; so the repeal of the prohibition and the renewal of the former permission; in a word, the reopening of the slave trade under the sanction of Congress, would in no long time change the character of domestic slavery, and deprive it of all color of just support. Africans openly seized and enslaved by violence would be worked with cruelty; humane masters would be driven in self-defense to practice the rigors of the mercenary and unscrupulous; the horrors of the old West Indian system would be reënacted; and the slavery in our Southern States to which its patrons now point with honest pride, would become all that its worst enemies declare it to be; the creature of inhuman fraud and violence, and a monstrous excrescence on Christian and civilized society. In this view of the case, it is plain that the evils which would enure to the Southern States on the reopening of the slave trade would be *infinitely* greater than those which are consequent on its secret and contraband character.

I have never yet seen an objection to the laws of the United States respecting the slave-trade, which was entitled, in my humble opinion, to a moment's consideration.

I have, indeed, seen it alleged that these laws make an unjust discrimination against slave-labor, inasmuch as they do not leave it, like other vendibles, to the law of demand and supply alone. But this objection is grounded, as it seems to me, on a total misapprehension; for the laws of the United States, I believe, make no such discrimination, but, on the contrary, leave slave labor to be bought and sold, to be let and hired, according to the law of supply and demand alone. The few restrictions (would to God they were greater and more numerous!) which exist, are merely designed to secure such humane treatment for slaves as is accorded to infants, or minors, who are put out to work by their guardians; and these proceed from the laws and enlightened public opinion of the States in which slavery is established. The Federal Government has nothing to do with slave labor, as an article of trade; and Congress has not passed, and can not pass, a discriminative law, either for or against it; has not attempted to regulate or touch it, in any way whatsoever, as an article of trade or commerce. The simple design of the laws of the United States respecting the slave-trade, is to prohibit piracy, and the importation into the ports under the jurisdiction of the United States, of persons piratically seized. The laws presume that the persons whose importation it forbids are not the property of those who hold and seek to import them, are not persons to whose labor any other man than themselves has a right; but that they are persons who have been stolen, or kidnapped, and forcibly, illegally, and unjustly, dragged from their homes; or who have been bought and kept for sale by those who have no shadow of right or title to hold them. And the laws justly presume this; for such is in fact the case with respect to those persons whom it is sought to import from a foreign country into any of the United States, to be sold as slaves. Prove that you have a just claim to the service of these persons, either by their own express consent, or by your having nurtured them on the condition that they should requite your nurture by their subsequent labor, or by your having bought them of others who had such just claim; prove this, I say, and then you may affirm, with at least a color of truth, and without audacity, that the laws of the United States are unjust to the South, by discriminating against slave-labor.

It would be easy to extend this argument, should an attempt be ever made to repeal the laws of the United States, which declare the slave-trade to be piracy. But I anticipate no such attempt. Slavery, considered as a domestic institution, is defensible on grounds of right and justice; and I see no reason to believe that the Southern States, while they continue in the Union, will surrender *this* ground of defense; as they clearly would do, were they to commit themselves to a measure which has no color of justice, and nothing to recommend it but a base cupidity, clothing itself in the garb of a hypocritical philanthropy. There may be men at the South who adopt, with an application of their own, the logic common at the North; who admit that the slave-trade is an evil, but think that it may be justified by what they fancy to be the necessity of their position, and who persuade themselves that they may, by this means, become instruments in the hands of Providence for civilizing and christianizing the benighted Africans: forgetting that Providence uses the vile as well as the good for the accomplishment of His purposes, and that they are but vile instruments in His hands whensoever, and under what pretext soever, they give their sanction to acts of injustice and oppression. These men, indeed, may agitate the repeal of the laws which declare the slave-trade to be piracy, but I can not believe that they express the settled sense and determination of the South, nor that the considerate men of the South will thus pronounce their own condemnation in the face of Christendom and at the bar of Eternal Justice. On the contrary, I believe that the South will unite with the North, and with nearly the same unanimity, in the belief that the laws of the United States making the slave-trade piracy are, equally with the laws which require fugitives from service to be delivered up to the parties to whom the service is due, declarative of the law of Nature, and consequently, for the matter of them, bound on the consciences of citizens by more awful sanctions than any which the municipal authority can impose.

CHAPTER XVII.

THE ARGUMENT FROM SCRIPTURE.

SLAVERY is a word of large extent. Prisoners and captives of war, criminals deprived of their liberty by process of law, persons piratically seized and reduced to bondage by violence, the serfs and villeins of other times and places, and servants for life in our own country—all come under the general denomination of *slaves*.

In this country we have come very naturally to appropriate the word *slavery* to that form of servitude which exists among ourselves. To know what the word *slavery* means in our use of it, we must first inquire what this form of servitude is; not what it is vaguely and in its accidents and abuses, but what it is precisely and in its essence. And the definition must be in accordance with facts; that is, it must express, not what slavery has been in other times and places, nor what it may be or might have been, but what it actually is in our own country and at the present time.

I have defined a slave to be *a person who is related to society through another person, called a master, to whom he owes reasonable service for life, and from whom he is entitled to receive support and protection.* This definition I believe to be in accordance with facts; in other words, I believe that those persons called *slaves* in our Southern States, are persons born on the soil and under such circumstances (circumstances not of our choosing but of God's ordering) that a debt of service is the very condition of their life. For we are not a nation of pirates and freebooters; we do not fit out vessels against an ignorant and unoffending people, to seize them and import them into our country, and reduce them to bondage. We have never done this; our mother country has never done it; no nation in modern Europe has done it. The work has been done by combinations of lawless men. And although Great Britain may have been remiss and tardy in restraining such violence, yet we, in this respect, have no ground of self-reproach. For, from the very beginning of our Confederacy, we took means to arrest this evil, and, as soon as practicable, enacted stringent laws, with a view to its suppression. More than fifty years—nearly two generations—have passed since these laws were in force. However much, therefore, we may lament and condemn the way in which slavery originated in our country, or the accessions (comparatively very small) which have since been made to it in the same way, yet we are not responsible for either; we gave no sanction to the former, and have done all that we could do to prevent the latter. We are, therefore, entitled to throw out of the account both the origin of slavery, and the few and accidental accessions it may receive from acts of violence which our laws prohibit; and to declare the slaves of our country to be, what in truth and fact they are, a class of persons born and grown on our soil, under an obligation of service which the laws of God and man require them to fulfill.

And, as we are not a nation of freebooters and pirates, so neither are we a barbarous and unchristian nation, permitting our people to exercise an absolute dominion over their subordinates and dependents. The laws of ancient Rome, which permitted a master to mutilate his slaves or put them to death by scores and hundreds at a time, for venial or, perhaps, only suspected offenses, are no criterion by which to judge of slavery in our Southern States. The power of masters is restrained among us both by law and by public opinion, within narrower, and but for the scandalous abuse of the right of transfer I would say, within reasonable limits; and hence we are entitled to regard the slaves that exist in our country, not as persons who are under the absolute power of their masters, but as persons who are subject to such coercion as is necessary to exact from them the service or labor they owe in return for their food and shelter.

In bringing the question to the arbitrament of Scripture, it is proper to distinguish that form of slavery for which we hold ourselves responsible, as, from all other forms, so, particularly, from that unjust deprivation of liberty which is effected by lawless violence.

When St. Paul enjoins *servants to obey their masters in all things*, he uses a word for servants (δουλοι), which comprises several sorts of persons restrained of liberty, and his precept is, consequently, to be taken in a sense suited to the condition of that class of servants to which it may be applied. On prisoners and captives held by lawless violence, or subject to absolute power, he enjoins obedience as an alleviation of their unhappy lot, which would be aggravated by resistance, and rendered more tolerable by patience and submission. On those who are bound to service, either for a term of time or for life, the precept must be understood to enjoin obedience according to the nature and condition of the service to which they are bound. To slaves of the former class, *i. e.*, to prisoners or captives who have been forcibly and unjustly seized and compelled to labor, at the oar for example, or in the mines, he would say, Obey your masters in all things, as becomes your sad condition, and make your chains as easy as you can, by your compliance and submission. To slaves of the latter class, *i. e.*, to persons who are justly bound to service, either for a term of time or for life, he would be understood to say: Obey your masters in all things according to the contract, express or implied, by which you are bound; or to use Bishop Fleetwood's paraphrase: "Behave yourselves to your masters as diligently and faithfully as you have promised them to do; *or by the custom of the place* (in which you live) *are presumed to have promised them.*"*

Now, if the slavery which exists in our country were upheld in violation of right and justice, although we might, after the example of the Apostles, inculcate on the slave the duty of patience and submission, yet we should be constrained to confess that the relation in which he stood was unnatural, and that the authority to which he was subjected was a usurpation. But, as I offer no apology for this kind of slavery, and have no need to press into my support those precepts which require of the slave what, indeed, is required of every man, patience and submission to the hardships of his lot, so I am not solicitous to repel the inferences which may be drawn from these precepts, in this sense of them, to show the injustice and impiety of slavery and slaveholders.

In appealing to the Scriptures, therefore, the question on which I would insist is, whether that form of slavery which I have defined, and which is known to exist in our country, be, or be not forbidden in the Scriptures? If it be, then all our reasonings in its defense are delusive, and must go for nothing; if it be not, then we are at liberty to uphold it; to regard the relation of master and slave, as it exists among us, as a lawful relation; and to consider it as fairly coming under those apostolical precepts which enjoin masters to be gentle and forbearing, and which enjoin servants to "obey their masters in all

* Works: Fol. Ed., p. 314.

things;" not in that sense which requires of them patience and submission under usurped authority, but in the other sense, which requires them to be diligent and faithful in a service which they are bound to perform.

Now, it is readily admitted that the form of slavery for which the American people are (a large portion of them directly) responsible, contains some features that are exceedingly repulsive to those who are accustomed to no other restraints of personal liberty than such as are imposed by the municipal law of the country in which they live. It gives the master, not indeed an absolute, but a large discretionary power over his servants; vests him with a right to their labor for life, and allows him to transfer this right to others; to invest any purchaser he may please with the same power over the bodies of his servants which he possesses himself. This certainly is a power liable to fearful abuses. It may seem to us antecedently probable that our blessed Lord, who came to reform the world, would never allow His followers to be clothed with such power; would forbid them, under all circumstances, to hold, or claim to hold a right to the service or labor of other men for life, and to the use of their natural liberty; or at least, if He suffered them to claim and hold this right, that He would not permit them to transfer it to a stranger for money. But we are in no sort judges beforehand of what it was fit for our Lord to do. It may, for aught we know, have seemed good to Him that some of His followers should be entrusted with this large power for their more effectual probation; for the development, possibly, of virtues which could not otherwise be manifested, and for a demonstration to the world of the efficacy of His gospel in restraining and regulating an authority which, before His time, had been abused beyond measure, and almost beyond belief. We are totally incompetent to judge beforehand what regulations it was proper for Him to make on this subject. Our inquiry is, or ought to be, simply into the *facts* of the case. Has our Lord in fact interdicted this sort of power and authority to His followers? Have His apostles done so? Did His Church do so in the age succeeding the apostles, when their instructions were remembered, and best understood?

Now, the *fact* is, that we have no prohibition of this sort, either from our Lord, or from His apostles, or from the ancient Church. Certainly there was no want of occasion or opportunity for such prohibition. The purchase and sale of the right to the use of men's labor and liberty, or property in men, as it is commonly, though vaguely called, had been permitted among the Hebrews, and was a matter cf every day practice among the Greeks and Romans; it could not possibly have escaped the observation of our Lord and His apostles, nor could its fearful abuses have been unknown to them. And yet the fact is, that there is nothing in the Scriptures of the New Testament which either expressly, or by implication, forbids it.

But the prohibition, though neither expressed or implied in the letter of the New Testament, is found by some in its spirit. There were evils, it is said, which Christ, for wise reasons, did not specifically and directly forbid, but left to be gradually restrained, and finally abolished by the silent and indirect influence of His gospel, or of those general principles which He has enunciated in His gospel. Such evils were polygamy, war, and slavery.

I shall not stop to question the legitimacy of the theory here implied. I shall admit, for argument's sake, that our Blessed Lord, while proclaiming all needful truth of a general nature, *reserved* some doctrine, of a more specific kind, which the world was not then in a temper to receive, and entrusted it to His apostles and their successors, to be afterwards unfolded and applied, in the shape of positive or negative precept, as men would be able to bear it. To be sure, this is commonly thought to be a very Papistical tenet; but the odium attached to the avowal of it will be considerably lightened when it is shared in common with Protestants of the Independent persuasion. But I must be permitted to question the applicability of the theory to the case in hand. I do not believe that our Lord reserved any doctrine to be authoritatively developed by Protestants in Women's Rights, Moral Reform, Temperance, or Anti-Slavery Societies. Whatever I may think of the developments of Rome and Trent (and they are not here in question),

I must be allowed to distrust those that come from Providence, Rhode Island, or from Oberlin, in whatever State or Territory Oberlin may be.

Let us look at the pretended parallels.

1. And first, it has become common to class polygamy and slavery together; and to argue that, as polygamy was anciently permitted by God, and afterwards abrogated, so slavery, though permitted under previous dispensations, was meant to expire under the Christian dispensation.

But where is the parallel? The marriage of one man to one woman, so that "they twain" should be "one flesh," was instituted at the beginning by God's *positive* law. Under the patriarchal and Jewish dispensations, the author of the law saw fit to dispense with its rigid observance. When Christ came into the world, He, in the name of His Father, annulled the temporary relaxation, and reaffirmed the original law.. By the original law, thus reaffirmed, divorce (save for the one cause) and polygamy are forbidden. The apostles provided for giving effect to this law, as promptly and stringently as could be, consistently with ties and obligations formed previously to the reënactment of the law. The extinction of polygamy, therefore, which rapidly followed, was not at all consequent on the indirect influence of the gospel, but was diretly consequent on the repeal of the relaxation and the reaffirmation of the original law.

But where is the original law which was dispensed in

order to the introduction of slavery? Where is the record of the dispensation? Where is the enactment or reënactment of any divine law prohibiting slavery? There is only one point of resemblance between the two cases; and that is, that polygamy and slavery were both permitted under the patriarchal and Mosaic dispensations. In all other respects the parallel fails; and the discontinuance of polygamy, in virtue of its express abrogation by the divine law, presents not a shadow of reason for expecting a discontinuance of slavery, as more agreeable to the gospel, without such abrogation.

2. The case of war is more in point. Christianity, by its indirect influence, *i. e.*, by quickening the principles of justice and benevolence, and binding men more closely in the bonds of a common humanity, has done much towards the prevention of *unjust* wars, and to mitigate the horrors of all wars. Admit the parallel, and what does it prove? Why, only this: that Christianity has done much to abrogate unjust slavery, and to lessen the evils of all slavery. But if the spirit of the gospel were to prevail universally, there would be no war; and hence, it is argued, there would be no slavery. But this by no means follows, for it is just here that the parallel fails. For, why would wars cease? Because there would be no injuries, and therefore no need even of a *just* war to redress them. But slavery, or that form of it which we are defending, is founded in the wants of human nature, or at least of human society; it

is not designed to defend us from violence, or to repel wrongs, but to diversify labor in ways consistent with innocence and justice, to coerce the vagrant and indolent to needful industry, to subsist the poor, to enable those who are unfit for bodily labor to devote their time and talents to the development of other sources of social wealth, and thus to bind together the head, and feet, and all the members of the political body in mutual concord. So that the spirit of the gospel, if it universally prevailed, though it should exterminate war, would but purify servitude.

3. Dismissing the alleged parallels, let us glance at the application of the argument to the case, for the illustration of which the parallels are adduced. The argument is that though the gospel does not directly forbid slavery, yet it provides for its extirpation by *indirect* influence; and the reasons assigned for this conclusion are such as follow.

In the first place it is contended that the Gospel proclaims *general principles*, the strict and faithful observance of which would be incompatible with the existence of slavery; as, for example, the gospel requires every man to love his neighbor as himself, and to do to others as he would have others to do to him.

Now, observe, we start with the admission that the gospel does not forbid the relation of master and slave, but, as respects the letter, permits it. Here, then, we are precipitated upon this extraordinary conclusion, viz., that a man can not obey, *in the fullness of their spirit*, the precepts of the Divine Lawgiver, without renouncing and subverting the very relation which those precepts are intended to regulate. That the precepts of love and equity enjoined on us by our Blessed Lord, have no such tendency as is supposed to impair and ultimately subvert the relation of master and slave, will be apparent if we take the precepts with those limitations which common sense requires, and which we give them when we apply them to every other relation of life. I am to love my neighbor, not in the same *measure* (which is impossible) but with the same *sincerity* that I love myself; and I am to do to others, not all that I might selfishly and lawlessly wish, but all that I could reasonably desire them, consistently with duty, to do to me, were I in their place and they in mine. I can see that the master, guided by these precepts, would have strong motives to the humane and generous treatment of his slaves; but I can not see that the spirit of the precepts, in any reasonable construction of them, is inconsistent with the perpetuity of the relation.

Another reason for the opinion that the gospel is indirectly adverse to slavery is, that, as the gospel diffuses light and knowledge, and slavery requires the soul to be kept in darkness, the two can not permanently coexist; and as the gospel is to triumph, slavery must succumb and perish.

Pray, of what gospel is this said? The gospel of

Christ and His apostles, or the gospel of my Lord Brougham and his schoolmasters? That the dissemination of "Useful Knowledge," as it is called, which supposes the art of reading to be the first step of human advancement, which multiplies books and tracts to save men from thinking and to nurse them in learned idleness,* or to fill their heads with false notions of human rights and fallacious theories of human society; filling their hearts, also, with discontent, envy, and hatred, and unfitting them, head and heart, for any humble and subordinate station, in which God's providence may have placed them; that this sort of light may lead to the extinction of slavery if permitted to penetrate it is like enough. But this sort of light is so far from being an indirect influence of Christianity, that it does not proceed from it at all, and, indeed, is as unlike it as is night to day. The light which Christ imparts is the knowledge of salvation; and for the propagation of this knowledge He has appointed His own means and His own agents; and *the art of reading* (however useful in its place) is not *the* means which He has appointed, nor is the school-

* "By this means," viz., "the great number of books and papers of amusement, which, of one kind or another, daily come in one's way," "time even in solitude is happily got rid of, without the pain of attention: *neither is any part of it more put to the account of idleness, one can scarce forbear saying, is spent with less thought than a great part of that which is spent in reading.*" So wrote the author of the Analogy (Preface to Sermons at the Rolls) more than a hundred years ago, and before the age of light literature had commenced.

master, although an important functionary in his way, *the* agent whom He has commissioned.

The knowledge which He requires in order to salvation is not abstruse or hard to be learned; it is diffused, indeed, in the Holy Scriptures, but may be thence collected, and summed up in brief rules of Faith, Devotion, and Charity, easy to be apprehended by the feeblest capacity. This knowledge, or the knowledge of these rules and rudiments, has from the beginning been taught *orally* to multitudes who were never able to learn it in any other way; and it is to this day imparted *orally* to all of us before we learn our letters, or are able to read the Bible. *Bene arguit, qui bene distinguit;* and I should suppose that the mere distinction between the knowledge of the kingdom of heaven and the knowledge of this world would be sufficient answer to the objection. For it can not, without absurdity, be believed that the light of the gospel, which teaches masters to be mild and gentle, and servants to be diligent and faithful, can indirectly, and in process of time, abolish a relation which it directly, now and always, cements.

Another reason for the opinion I am combating is, that the gospel forbids cruelty, oppression, and impurity, and all the other evils which are the concomitants of slavery, and make it the "sum of human villainies," and that, therefore, it must tend indirectly to its extirpation.

I answer that, if these evils are *inseparable* from slavery, then we have a right to expect that slavery would have been *directly* forbidden in the gospel; and since it is not so forbidden, we have the right to infer that these evils are separable from it; and if separable, then their restraint and inhibition can only tend to strip slavery of its abuses, and thus to reform the institution, and not to subvert it.

But the crowning argument remains; viz., that, after the establishment of Christianity, and under its benign influence, slavery became gradually extinct.

This reasoning, I apprehend, is no better than the *post hoc, propter hoc* logic, which is sometimes maliciously charged on the medical profession. The drug is administered, and the patient recovers; *ergo* the drug has cured him! The truth is, in my opinion, that Christianity had no more to do with the decay of slavery in the Roman empire, than it had with its extirpation in our Northern States. In both cases slavery was abandoned because it did not pay. In the New England and Middle States, where the produce of the earth is slowly yielded and hardly obtained, and where the cold climate braces and disposes the white for work, while it enervates and incapacitates the negro, it cost the master more to feed and rear his slaves than their labor was worth; and hence they who owned negro slaves at the North sold them to the South, where their labor would be worth more than their keeping; not refusing to accept (why should they?) whatever credit they could get for philanthropy, and not grudging to send with or after each bill of sale, a lecture or short tract on the sin of holding property in man. So in the Roman empire. While the rage for conquest prevailed, the bulk of the people were employed in wars abroad, and left their work at home to be done by slaves; and as their habits were frugal, and their slaves were valued only for their labor, they could much better afford to keep them than to relinquish their plunder in foreign countries. But when the rage for conquest had ceased, the bulk of the people, deprived of warlike employment, were compelled to turn their attention to agriculture and mechanical pursuits; and as luxury had now increased, and the rich and opulent affected more than ever the elegancies and refinements of life, they put their slaves to such sorts of work as required not merely muscle but skill and training; hence slave-labor became more expensive, and free labor cheaper; and when matters came to that pass, that it cost more to rear and train the slave for his work than his work was worth, then slavery did not pay; and when slavery ceased to pay, it died out, the gospel contributing nothing, directly or indirectly, to its decadence.

The upshot of the matter is, as it seems to me, that Christianity neither enjoins nor forbids slavery, but leaves men entirely free, so that they restrain themselves within the bounds of justice and rectitude, either to discourage and abolish it, or to establish and uphold it, as the public good may require.

The plan of my work does not require me to do more

than establish this negative conclusion. A strong affirmative argument, indeed, might easily be made to show that the Scriptures, both of the Old and New Testament, expressly recognize and sanction slavery; but this argument has been so often and so luminously stated, and, indeed, the fact is so apparent on the very face of the Scriptures, that I deem it quite superfluous to swell my pages with references and quotations designed to establish it.* Besides, the aim of my argument has been to show that that form of servitude which exists under the laws of some of our States, and under the Constitution of the United States, is consistent with natural justice; and if the argument is sound, slavery must stand unless the Scriptures forbid it. That "the New Testament contains no *precept* prohibitory of slavery" is expressly affirmed by the ablest of the New England abolitionists; and what they insist on is that the prohibition, though not given in any *precept*, is yet contained in the *principles* of the New Testament, of course as developed and applied by themselves. Their arguments are misty and confused, and it is about as hard to seize and explain them, as it would be to bottle and analyze the dense fog that sometimes hangs over their coast. But, as far as I could catch their meaning, I have given and answered it;

* For a synopsis of the scriptural argument the reader is referred to "Slaveholding not Sinful," by Samuel S. How, D.D., of New Brunswick, and for sale by R. & R. Brinkerhoof, 103 Fulton Street, New York.

and the result is, I think, that the gospel, neither directly nor indirectly, neither by its precepts nor principles, makes slavery a sin; in short, that it contains not a seed or germ to serve them for their new Protestant "development of Christian doctrine."

Before I leave this topic, I wish to guard the reader against a mistake into which he may be led by an equivocation of words. The apostles admitted into the communion of the Christian Church, the "bond," as well as the free. From the apostles' time, to the accession of Constantine in the fourth century, not to go later, it is matter of undoubted history, that slaves, by which word I mean persons that were owned by others under the laws of the Empire, that were kept for labor and were liable to be bought and sold, formed a numerous class in the Christian Church; they were "called," in common with others, from among the Gentiles, and remained, according to the apostolic precedent, "in the vocation wherein they were called." One of the Apostolic Canons (the eighty-second in Beveridge's collection, and seventy-third in Johnson's) declares: "We do not permit slaves to be ordained to the clergy, without consent of their masters, and to the provocation of their owners; for this would be to the subversion of families; but if a slave do appear worthy of being ordained even priest or bishop, and their owners give way to it, by making them free, and dismissing them from their houses, let it be done."* Bingham, in adverting to this canon, remarks that "the servants referred to were originally tied by birth or purchase to their patrons' or masters' service;" and assigns as a reason for the canon that "no man was to be defrauded of his right under pretense of ordination."† The same author, as above quoted,‡ tells us: "The same power and right which parents had over their children, masters had over their slaves: and for this reason no slave could marry without the consent of his master." In the eleventh book of his Antiquities, which treats of the rites and customs observed in the administration of baptism, he relates, "that in the examination of the several qualifications of those that offered themselves to baptism, one part of the inquiry was, 'whether they were slaves, or freemen?' If they were slaves to a heathen, they were only taught their obligations to please their master, that the word of God might not be blasphemed; and the master had no further concern in their baptism, as being himself an infidel; but if the master were a Christian, then the testimony of the master was first to be required concerning the life and conversation of his slave, before he could be admitted to the privilege of baptism. If he gave a laudable account of him, he was received; if otherwise, he was rejected, till he approved himself to his master."§ From all

* Johnson's translation, *Vade Mecum*, vol. ii., p. 36.

† Vol. i. p. 487, Pitman's Edition. ‡ *Vide Supra*, chap. xiii., p. 212.

§ Vol. iii., p. 488.

which it appears incontrovertibly that slavery, in the best days of the Christian Church, was not accounted to be a sin or disgrace. Neither was the slave, *as such*, regarded as an object of commiseration. The horrible phantasm of "property in man" did not scare the plain piety of these early Christians, any more than it perplexed the plain sense of their heathen neighbors. Slaves were respected according to their condition in life, and their behaviour in that condition. Some of them were very ignorant, and had a hard lot; and others of them were intelligent and prosperous. Onesimus, the absconding slave whom St. Paul sent back to his master, is said, by some of the ancients, to have earned his freedom by his good conduct, and to have been made Bishop of Colosse. St. Luke, the Evangelist, is believed by Grotius, and others, to have been a slave in the family of the *Lucilli*, and to have taken from them his diminutive name of *Luke*. However this be, I believe I am right in saying that slaves, *as such, i. e.*, persons who were owned, and liable to be sold under the laws of the Empire, were not regarded as objects of ignominy or compassion.

And yet we are sometimes told that the sympathies and charities of the Primitive Church were often excited in behalf of persons in slavery, and that large contributions were made by the benevolent to purchase their freedom. In particular, the thrilling letter of St. Cyprian, Bishop of Carthage, to the Numidian bishops, deploring the miseries of slavery, and sending *a hundred thousand sesterces* (equal to between three and four thousand dollars), contributed by the churches under his charge, to ransom some unhappy slaves in Numidia out of the house of bondage, is quoted, with marvelous effect, to show the horrors of slavery, and the sentiments of compassion with which it was regarded in the Primitive Church. How reconcile this with our previous statement, that slavery, as such, was not an object of commiseration, and with the natural inference from the statement, that the Christians of that day were not commonly called upon to contribute money to enable slaves to change their state or condition in life?

"We, Christians," says St. Cyprian, "are all incorporated together as one body; and not only the motives of humanity, but those of our holy religion ought to excite and quicken our endeavors for redeeming our brethren from their slavery." He observes, moreover, that "as many as have been baptized into Christ, have put on Christ;" and that for this reason we ought to behold Christ in the persons of slaves, who are our brethren, and redeem Him [in their persons] from His slavery, who redeemeth us from the death to which we were obnoxious; * * * that he who redeemed us by His cross and passion, may Himself be redeemed with our money." What, then, would the venerable Bishop of Carthage say, were he now alive, to the pious abolitionist who should quote his language to excite the commiseration of

Christians, for the hard lot of our Southern slaves? Why, he would rebuke him, and hold him up to the scorn of men as an impudent falsifier! The letter to the Numidian bishops has no relation to slaves, in the common sense of the word. Under the negligent administration of Gallus, says Dr. Marshall, the barbarous nations bordering on the confines of the Roman dominions in Africa, made frequent incursions upon their neighbors in the Roman territory, and *carried off many captives;* on whose behalf the bishops, in those parts, had written to our author [St. Cyprian] for contributions to assist in redeeming them; and received from him this letter in answer."

That the reader may see how easy it is to cheat with ambiguous words, and with quotations wrested from their context, I annex the first paragraph of this noble letter from Marshall's Cyprian, Vol. II. p. 176.

"Cyprian to his brethren Januarius, Maximus, Proculus, Victor, Modianus, Nemesianus, Nampulus, and Honoratus, sendeth greeting.

"I read over, my dearest brethren, the letter which you sent me, concerning the captivity of our brothers and sisters, with a compassion and concern equal to what you wrote it with; for who can withhold his tears from flowing out upon such dreadful calamities? Or who would not consider the misfortune of his brethren as, in some measure, his own? Especially, when he shall reflect upon what the apostle St. Paul hath said upon this subject; 'Whether one member suffer, all the members suffer with it; or one member rejoice, all the members rejoice with it.' And again; 'Who is weak, and I am not weak?' We, therefore, should look upon the captivity of our brethren as a state of bondage to ourselves; since we are all incorporated together as one body; and not only the motives of *humanity*, but those of our holy *religion*, ought to excite and quicken our endeavors for redeeming our brethren from slavery: for the apostle St. Paul, having in another place put the question; 'know ye not that ye are the temple of God, and that the Spirit of God dwelleth in you?' if the rules of *charity* did not oblige us to assist our brethren in such extremity, yet we ought to consider here, that they are the temples of God, which thus are taken captive; that therefore we should not, by our neglect and indolence, suffer them to continue long under their confinement; but should rather labor with all our industry and application to gain the favor of Christ our Judge, Lord, and God, by our good offices towards them. The same apostle St. Paul hath told us that, 'as many of us as have been baptized into Christ, have put on Christ.' Wherefore we should behold Christ in the persons of our captive brethren, and redeem Him from His slavery, who redeemeth us from the death to which we were obnoxious; that He who hath taken us out of the jaws of the devil, and dwelleth and abideth in us, may (Himself) be taken out of the hands of the barbarians; and that He who redeemed us by His cross and passion, may Himself be redeemed with our money; who, perhaps, hath permitted this misfortune to befall our brethren, that He thence might try the power of our faith, and whether we will do in the case of others, what we should desire to have done for ourselves, if we were captives in the hands of these barbarians. For who, with any sense about him of humanity and mutual benevolence, would not, if he be a father, imagine those his children, who are there in slavery? Or if he be a husband, would not entertain those sentiments of tenderness and concern for the honor of his marriage-bed, which he could not but entertain, if his own wife were there?"

CHAPTER XVIII.

CONCLUSION.

Having now brought my argument to a close, I beg to direct the reader's attention to a brief review of the positions which I have endeavored to establish, and to the course of action which they naturally suggest in reference to the present state of our country.

Reverting to the point from which we started, the era of the great men who inaugurated our independence, we find our people united in the same religion. Our social relations were not derived from heathen prescription, nor modeled on Utopian theories, but were those which we had inherited from Christian ancestors. Our government made no provision for the uniform inculcation of the fundamental principles of religion on which it was founded, but threw itself entirely on the good sense of the people; and while undertaking to administer their political affairs, left to them the whole responsibility of maintaining the principles on which its whole machinery, the civilization which it had adopted, the social order and relations which it protected—in a word, its very life and being depended for support.

Thus we set out on our career as a civilized and Christian people, according to the highest standard of civilization to which mankind had then arrived, and with such principles of religion as afforded a broad and ample foundation for a healthy Christian society. After the lapse of more than half a century one of the social relations, protected by government, was assailed as barbarous and anti-Christian; and the Constitution, for the protection which it afforded to this relation was also denounced as barbarous and anti-Christian, and as needing to be reformed to a higher civilization and a purer religion. Government had provided no means for its own security, either moral or physical, either preventive or remedial, against assaults of this nature: it permitted an unlimited freedom of speech and of the press, and authorized no means of instruction for their guidance; it made it the duty of no man or of any order of men to define and inculcate those fundamental principles of morality and religion on which all human society rests for support; it gave full swing to assailants and agitators, and men who in any previous age and under almost any other government on earth would have been compelled to choose between a bridle for their lips and a halter for their necks, were suffered to go on from month to month, and from year to year, and denounce the Constitution under which they lived as "a covenant with death and an agreement with hell." By their eloquent but superficial harangues the agitators captivated the people; the politicians were not slow to use the public opinion which the agitators created; they joined and outstripped them in sophistical appeals to the people in behalf of that universal equality and those natural rights which the Declaration of Independence proclaimed, and of which they thought, or affected to think, that the slavery in our Southern States was a violation. Nay, they went farther, and raised their voice in the halls of legislation to arraign the Constitution itself for inconsistency with that "Higher Law," of which they knew, or ought to have known, that it is, on the very point on which they have arraigned it, a true and infallible exponent. To protect itself against assaults of this nature, government confided wholly to the intelligence of the people and their ability to comprehend and apply the fundamental principles on which the relation that was assailed, in common with the other relations of human society, rest for support. And the question was and is, for it is still undecided, whether the confidence is misplaced: whether the people will continue to chase the phantoms held up to them by stationary pulpiteers and itinerant demagogues, or whether they will justify the wisdom of their fathers and reject the fallacies and sophistries by which they are taught to use the Declaration of Independence for the subversion of their government, and the Gospel of Christ for the division of His Church.

The effect of these repeated and long-continued onslaughts on slavery has been to excite the passions of the South, and to extort from them more of denunciation than argument; although the latter has not been wanting. And this is perfectly natural. By the very constitution of our nature we are led to believe in the truth and justice of the religious and social institutions which are the foundation of our dearest hopes and interests, before we are able to develop the logical grounds of our belief. Hard, indeed, would be the lot of Christians, if they had no firm and solid ground for their faith until they had learned from the schools to refute the sophistries of Hume, and to estimate, at their true value, the sneers of Gibbon or the sarcasm of Voltaire. The rich never think of looking beyond their title-deeds to justify the tenure of houses and lands which they have bought with their money, or inherited from their fathers; and not one in ten thousand of them is able to explain the origin of property, nor to give a logical answer to those who from the right of the people to make their own laws would infer their right to adjust property on a new basis. An agrarian party at the North, if numerous and successful, would provoke from the rich among us more imprecations than syllogisms. So at the South. Men who have been born in a society of which slavery is an element; who have come peaceably and honorably into the possession of slaves, and are assured of their attachment; who are accustomed to the idea of property in servile labor, and esteem it no degradation, but build upon it their hopes of worldly prosperity; these men, I say, believe in the essential justice of their system of society, and of their title to property under the laws of the States in which they live, before they learn logically to explain and develop the grounds of their belief. It is idle to say that Mr. Calhoun has revolutionized their sentiments and taught them a doctrine which they never entertained before. The change of opinion which has undoubtedly taken place in the South on this subject, has been the consequence of the transition of slavery from its violent original to its settled condition in society. Nature itself has made the change, and neither Mr. Calhoun nor any other man could do more than direct attention to the facts consequent on the change, and give logical form and expression to the conviction which those facts had before implicitly wrought in the mind of Southern society. It ought, therefore, to be no matter of surprise that our Southern brethren, when the very foundations of their social structure were attacked on grounds of morality and religion, were more prompt to resent the attacks than to refute them.

As long as the anti-slavery element depended for its practical development on the Abolitionists, it could do no harm to the government. For the Abolitionists were honest and straightforward; they believed slavery to be a sin and disgrace, and turned their batteries at once on the Constitution which protected it. By this extravagance they disgusted the more sedate opponents of slavery, who joined in sneering at them as men of "one idea," and thus (for the apostles themselves were men of "one idea") strengthened their moral influence, while they discountenanced their political measures. But when the politician thrust his sickle into the Abolition harvest, and a party was organized which had for one of its objects to oppose and restrain slavery only by constitutional and conservative methods, a fair opportunity was presented for testing the sense of the people. The contest was waged with "polygamy and slavery, twin relics of barbarism," for a motto; and the result showed that the anti-slavery feeling, far from being limited to the Abolitionists, was predominant in the Northern mind. What ends anti-slavery sentiment, working only in a constitutional way, could have accomplished, it is needless to inquire; since the South, rather than await the experiment, have resorted to secession and revolution. And the question now is, how to reinstate ourselves in the condition in which we were before the moral and social character of slavery was introduced into our party politics.

I concur, in general, with those who think that the best way to recover our former harmony (if, indeed, the recovery be possible), is to copy the example of our fathers; to guard the government which they established from all influences which tend to warp it from its original design, and to seek to transmit to our children the same heritage, pure and undefiled, which we have received from them.

There are two ways, however, in which this laudable aim may be pursued. The one is, to plant ourselves on the principles on which our fathers stood, and to apply them, in the exercise of a sound discretion, to the solution of new problems; and the other is, to take some opinion which they entertained on some measure which they adopted, and to carry out the opinion and to imitate the measure without due regard to the principles by which they were governed, or the new circumstances by which we are surrounded.

There can be no doubt that the founders of our government were, on political and economical grounds, opposed to slavery, and that they wished to get rid of it. But their opinions and wishes were controlled by principles from which they never swerved. *Their love of justice* was stronger than their aversion to slavery; and it taught them to do no violence to the bond which tied the slave to his master, nor to seek to deprive the master of his right to the slave's labor. *Their love of union* was stronger than their aversion to slavery; for it led them to adopt a Constitution which protected slavery in States which had no intention to abolish it. They indeed prohibited slavery in the Northwestern territory; but no one State opposed the prohibition; the South concurred in the measure with the North; and the only dissenting vote was from a representative of New York. In carrying out their very laudable opinions and wishes in this respect, they did no violence to the great principles which governed them—the love of justice, and the love of union.

After the lapse of seventy years, the settlement of another territory is brought in question. We at the North desire, very naturally, that this territory also should be dedicated to freedom. And in favor of this measure we have the example of our fathers in a similar case, and their opinions of the deleterious influence of slavery. Let us revere their example, and cherish their opinions. But let us remember also that our circumstances are different from those in which they were placed. The territory is farther South. The Slave States, instead of concurring with us, oppose the measure which we desire to carry. And the Slave States are more populous now than they were then; the population of some of them having nearly reached that point of density,* where the maintenance of the slave is of more value than his labor, and where, consequently, slavery dies a natural death; the owner himself being glad to be relieved of his burthen. In proportion as this point is approached, the value of slave labor depreciates; and the density of population is increased in proportion as its expansion is prevented. In view, then, of our altered circumstances, let us be governed by the great principles on which our

* The result of Professor Tucker's careful and elaborate investigation is, that the depreciation in the value of slave labor begins when the population reaches the number of fifty persons to the square mile. See *Progress of the United States in Population and Wealth*, chapter xiii. By GEORGE TUCKER.

fathers acted—love of Justice, love of Union. Let us love free territory much, justice and union more.

Our fathers foresaw the evils which threatened the Union, and they have marked out the course by which they hoped to avoid them. That course contemplates two fixed and uncompromising principles of action: 1, the toleration of domestic slavery on grounds both of justice and expediency: and 2, the resolute prohibition and, as far as possible, annihilation of the slave-trade. Can we do better than adhere to the policy which their wisdom prescribed? If the Union is dissolved and a Southern confederacy formed, the slave-trade will probably be reopened. Will that be any comfort to the North? If we can maintain the Union, and uphold its laws against the slave-trade, at the expense of letting domestic slavery alone, and suffering it to be governed by the laws of population and labor, is it not better for us to do so? Do not the wisdom and example of our fathers compel us to tolerate the less evil, for the sake of avoiding the greater?

Before we adopt measures to circumscribe slavery, and thus to accelerate its extinction, and bring it about at an earlier period than is prescribed to it by the natural laws of population and labor, ought we not to be prepared with some feasible and effective plan for extending to free colored people that moral, religious, and physical protection to which, while we exclude them from citizenship and from social and political equality, they are by the

LAW OF NATURE entitled at our hands? Even under our present system of servitude, with all its abuses, the colored people that live in it are, as a general rule, cared for in respect both to their spiritual and temporal necessities. If we take measures which tend, even remotely, to deprive them of this protection, and accompany them with no provision for admitting them to social and political equality with ourselves, we expose them to temptations to vagrancy, intemperance and vice, which experience shows that they will not resist. We shall leave them, as we have left the original inhabitants of our land, to dwindle away and die out for want of the stimulants and motives which human nature demands to excite it to the pursuit of industry, intelligence, and virtue. A truly philanthropic heart, really concerned for the welfare of this unhappy portion of mankind, can derive no comfort from this prospect.

In the pursuit of a higher civilization and a purer religion than our fathers have bequeathed to us, a relentless war has been raged against one relation of society. Suppose the assailants succeed, and either abolish slavery, or, by breaking up the Union, relieve themselves of the obligation which now presses on them to enlighten the consciences, and reform the lives of the benighted South. What next? Their mission is to raise the *individual* above the State, and to convince him that government is instituted, not for the common good of society, and the harmonious development of its manifold and diversified interests, but for *his* elevation and improvement; and their mission will be unfulfilled unless every individual man and woman is made the equal of every other in all the advantages which government, on their theory of it, is designed to confer. Not only must slaves have equal civil rights with their masters, but women must have an equal share in government with men, and the poor an equal share of property with the rich. Here is the point of antagonism between the genius of modern civilization and the law of Nature and of CHRIST. Nature teaches that government is instituted for the common good, and for the individual in subordination to the common good, and the history of all orderly society, from the beginning of the world, illustrates and confirms her teaching; and Christianity, both in fact and by precept, binds each member of society to every other, and makes all subject to the head; while the genius of modern civilization builds the State on the idea of the individual and tends to exalt and to benefit him at the expense of the State. Revolutionary France is a type of its extreme development where it is not tempered and restrained by the prescriptions of reason and the authority of revelation; and without these divine restraints, all the measures of pretended reform and progress, which it inaugurates, are essentially anti-Christian; none the less so because Satan, in order to accomplish them, transforms himself into an angel of light. To what extent they foreshadow the great ANTI-CHRIST, which is to concentrate all the elements of infidelity in one terrific power of destruction, might be worth considering, if men were in a temper to consider so serious a subject.

The views which I have advocated, in respect to slavery, can only affect our intercourse with our brethren at the South, and our estimate of their condition. They can not, by any possibility, even if they were generally adopted, lead to the reinstatement of slavery at the North; but they will dispose us to feel and to act more kindly towards those to whose care Providence has intrusted the large portion of our fellow-countrymen and fellow-christians, who now live in that state of servitude which nothing but our own pride and folly makes disreputable in our sight. They will not only regain for us the now alienated affections of our Southern brethren, but they will restore to the bosoms of their families that "domestic tranquillity," that mutual good-will and confidence, of which the present opinions at the North have, in a measure, deprived them. By allaying the jealousy, and healing the wounded pride of the master, they will promote the comfort, and secure the mild treatment of the slave, and remove the impediments which, in some places and to some extent, have impeded his liberation. They furnish, moreover, a solid ground for the inculcation of the mutual obligations and duties, which grow out of one of the most important relations in human society. I do not urge these considerations as proofs of the theory of slavery, which I have advocated, but as reasons which should secure for it, if it be not erroneous, a hold upon our affections. If others take delight in maintaining the opposite theory, and spreading before the public distorted facts and exaggerated statements to sustain it, I must leave them to pursue the bent of their own minds. But, for my own part, to accommodate to my use the familiar words of an ancient philosopher on another subject,* if I err in this opinion, viz., that the slavery, which exists under our laws, is founded in justice, and not in violence—I gladly err; nor do I wish, while our Union lasts, to be robbed of an error, which fills me with kindly and benevolent regard toward all its members; and if—which God in His mercy forbid!—our Union should perish, I would still rejoice in an error, which has saved me from the guilt of having promoted its dissolution, and which will continue to make all who accept it at the North of one heart, even after they shall have ceased to be of one country, with the South.

Adieu, dear reader, and may you ever be as fit and prepared to receive, as the writer is disposed and desirous to invoke on you and yours, the peace and benediction of ALMIGHTY GOD!

* Quod si in hoc erro, quod animos hominum immortales esse credam, libenter erro; nec mihi hunc errorem, quo delector, dum vivo, extorqueri volo: sin mortuus, ut quidam minuti philosophi censent, nihil sentiam, non vereor, ne hunc errorem meum mortui philosophi irrideant.—*De Senectute.*

APPENDIX.

A.

Appended is the original of the passage from Pliny, quoted in the ninth chapter, and accidentally omitted in its proper place: it forms the proem to his seventh book.

Mundus, et in eo terræ, gentes, maria, insignes insulæ, urbes ad hunc modum se habent. Animantium in eodem natura nullius prope partis contemplatione minor est, siquidem omnia exequi humanus animus queat. Principium jure tribuetur homini, cujus causa videtur cuncta alia genuisse natura, magna et sæva mercede contra tanta sua munera; ut non sit satis æstimare, parens melior homini, an tristior noverca fuerit. Ante omnia unum animantium cunctorum alienis velat opibus: cæteris varie tegumenta tribuit, testas, cortices, coria, spinas, villos, setas, pilos, plumam, pennas, squamas, vellera. Truncos etiam arboresque cortice, interdum gemino, a frigoribus et calore tutata est. Hominem tantum nudum et in nuda humo, natali die abjicit ad vagitus statim et ploratum, nullumque tot animalium aliud ad lacrymas, et has protinus vitæ principio. At, Hercule, risus præcox ille et celerrimus ante quadrigesimum diem nulli datur. Ab hoc lucis rudimento, quæ ne feras quidem inter nos genitas, vincula excipiunt, et omnium membrorum nexus: itaque infeliciter natus jacet manibus pedibusque devinctis, flens, animal cæteris imperaturum; et a suppliciis vitam auspicatur, unam tantum ob culpam, qua natum est. Heu dementiam ab iis initiis existimantium ad superbiam se genitos! Prima roboris spes, primumque temporis munus quadrupedi similem facit. Quando homini incessus? quando vox? quando firmum cibis os? quandiu palpitans vertex, summæ inter cuncta animalia imbecillitatis indicium? Jam morbi, totque medicinæ contra mala excogitatæ, et hæ quoque subinde novitatibus victæ. Cætera sentire naturam suam, alia pernicitatem usurpare, alia præpetes volatus, alia nare: hominem nihil scire, nihil, sine doctrina, non fari, non ingredi, non vesci: breviterque non aliud naturæ sponte, quam flere. Itaque multi extitere, qui non nasci optimum censerent, aut quam ocyssime aboleri. Uni animantium luctus est datus, uni luxuria, et quidem innumerabi libus modis, ac per singula membra: uni ambitio, uni avaritia, uni immensa vivendi cupido, uni superstitio, uni sepulturæ cura, atque etiam post se de futuro. Nulli vita fragilior, nulli rerum omnium libido major, nulli pavor confusior, nulli rabies acrior. Denique cœtera animantia in suo genere probe degunt: congregari videmus, et stare contra dissimilia: leonum feritas inter se non dimicat; serpentium morsus non petit serpentes; ne maris quidem belluæ ac pisces, nisi in diversa genera, sæviunt. At, Hercule, homini plurima ex homine sunt mala.

B.

In the Chapter on the "Rendition of Fugitives from Labor," I have expressed the opinion that the people are not required, by the law of 1850, to assist in the recovery of the fugitive, but merely to assist the officers of justice to defeat any factious opposition which may be made to the recovery, the officer himself being supposed to be able to execute the law in case of the fugitive being the only person to resist it. Such is my construction of the law; but, that the reader may judge of the matter for himself, I annex the clause referred to. The point is of no importance to the main argument, which is designed to establish the principle of the law rather than to defend its particular provisions:

An Act to amend the Act respecting Fugitives, etc., passed Sept. 18, 1850.

"§ 5. * * * * * And the better to enable the said Commissioners, when thus appointed, to execute their duties faithfully and efficiently, in conformity with the requirements of the

Constitution of the United States and of this Act, they are hereby authorized and empowered, within their counties respectively, to appoint, in writing, under their hands, any one or more suitable persons, from time to time, to execute all such warrants and other process as may be issued by them in the lawful performance of their respective duties; with authority to such Commissioners, or the persons to be appointed by them, to execute process as aforesaid, to summon and call to their aid the bystanders, or posse comitatus of the proper county, when necessary to ensure a faithful observance of the clause of the Constitution referred to, in conformity with the provisions of this Act; and all good citizens are hereby commanded to aid and assist in the prompt and efficient execution of this law, whenever their services may be required, as aforesaid, for that purpose; and said warrants shall run, and be executed by said officers, anywhere in the State within which they are issued." * * *

THE END.

www.ingramcontent.com/pod-product-compliance
Lightning Source LLC
LaVergne TN
LVHW020223110826
845151LV00003B/812

* 9 7 8 1 4 2 5 5 3 1 6 8 3 *